Nigerian Dwarf Goat.

Keeping Nigerian Dwarf Goats as Pets.

Nigerian Dwarf Goat book for daily care, pros and cons, raising, training, feeding, housing and health.

by

Peter Patterdale

Published by: IMB Publishing

Table of Contents

Chapter 1 - Introduction

Nigerian Dwarf goats are absolutely adorable! They don't take up much room and they don't weigh as much as full sized goats. With that in mind you don't need as much space for them or to feed them as much. They get along well with people and make wonderful pets.

They are quite entertaining too, due to their behaviors and social skills. The young ones love to play and to explore. Even older miniature goats enjoy jumping and playing games. They are very intelligent too so they are able to explore their environment and learn quickly.

Many people don't realize it, but you can actually train Nigerian Dwarf goats to walk on a leash if you want to. You can also teach them simple commands such as to come to you, to sit, and to lie down.

They are very social animals and they enjoy being touched. Rubbing their stomach or patting them on the head can make them feel very happy and assist with the bonding process. They do need daily interaction with each other to thrive, though. They will become very lonely and even suffer from depression.

A single goat is a lonely goat so if you get one, be ready to get at least a pair! More than that is going to make them happier but it means more work for you. If they don't thrive socially they will produce less milk and they are less likely to mate. Therefore, you need to make a commitment to owning two or more Nigerian Dwarf goats.

There are so many good things to say about Nigerian Dwarf goats. Yet it isn't all fun and games with them, as they require plenty of care on a daily basis. It is important to understand that side of it too before you get any of them. Perhaps you are considering these goats as pets, for their milk, or for breeding.

You need to have a safe place for them to live and plenty of food for them to thrive. They need to have the right nutrition in order for them to grow and remain healthy. The wrong food can result in them not producing enough milk.

Understanding the cost and the care involved with these goats is very important. You will have the initial startup costs of getting your shelter ready for them. Depending on where you live you may already have something to start with. Reinforcing it and upgrading it to fit the needs of these goats is important.

Of course you have your cost of buying the goats too. This cost will vary based on a variety of factors. Such information will be covered in its own chapter due to the amount of information to think about. I do encourage you to take your time with buying and only to buy from certified breeders.

The cost of food for them is something you need to budget for all year long. There is no compromising when it comes to the food and the extras for your goats. If you can't afford this with ease in your budget it may not be a good idea for you to own them.

There is also the cost of caring for their health. Nigerian Dwarf goats are going to need vaccines each year. They also need health care to prevent worms and other concerns. Should your goats become sick, you may need to spend hundreds of dollars for vet care and medication to get them well again.

Weighing the pros and cons before you dive in is important. Being well informed about what it will take to keep them healthy and happy is essential. If you live on a tight budget you also have to think about the daily costs involved for their care. If you can afford them and you have the time for them, you will be well rewarded with their affection and the milk they produce.

My Love of Animals

I smile all the time when I think about my childhood. We lived on a farm and I had a deep love for animals from an early age. I can remember going out in the morning with my mom to feed the goats and other animals. She was very patient with me. By the time I was a youngster I was doing such chores on my own. Even though we had various types of animals, the Nigerian Dwarf goats always had a special place in my heart.

I would spend extra time with them when I did chores in the morning and at night. I would beg my mom to let me stay up late if one of our goats was about to have her babies. I would also spend time with the goats playing and chasing them.

I know some people think goats will chew on anything and eat everything but that isn't really the case. Keeping items out of sight that they could chew on or eat is important. I have never had goats eat clothing or objects so you don't have to be too concerned about it as long as you use some common sense.

We did have a goat that liked to chew on my daughter's hair! I think it may have thought it was some type of treat – the color could have passed for hay! I will tell you that story in more detail though in the segment about training your Nigerian Dwarf goats.

I didn't mind the chores growing up, it was my chance to spend time with the animals. It gave me a strong sense of responsibility and respect for animals. I have passed that along to my own children and they adore our goats.

I have always loved to watch them engage in their behaviors and interact with each other. If you aren't an animal lover, it doesn't make any sense for you to own Nigerian Dwarf goats. They are quite social and they are very entertaining but they are also a huge responsibility.

I was lucky enough to grow up on a farm with my parents who were excellent with all of our animals. They had the right skills, offered them the right food, and we had plenty of room for them. Sadly, I have seen people neglect these goats and other pets. It just doesn't sit well with me because they deserve so much better.

Now, you may not have grown up on a farm, but that doesn't mean you can't learn how to care for Nigerian Dwarf goats successfully. A good family friend of ours is as city oriented as they come! However, she came to visit for a week and fell in love with our goats. Her husband wasn't sold on the idea but over time he came to realize she was very passionate about it. Today she has three of them and sends us pictures often!

About Nigerian Dwarf Goats

If you plan to own these amazing animals, I recommend you understand the background history about them. The Nigerian Dwarf goat is a dairy goat, a miniature breed. They originated in West Africa but were imported to other areas around the world in the 1970s. Today, they are considered to be a rare breed of goat with the American Minor Breeds Conservancy.

That fact alone means it is harder to gain access to them for just anyone. There is a high demand for these goats. As a result, breeders are able to charge a premium for them. Of course if you plan to have these goats for your own breeding and resell business then you can already see how it would be a profitable investment. There are approximately 25,000 of them according to the registry but the numbers are steadily increasing.

To be clear, this is a book about these goats as pets and how to enjoy their milk. We will touch on the topic of breeding in a chapter but that isn't our focus. There are plenty of books out there about breeding Nigerian Dwarf goats but this isn't going to be one that offers you more than just the basics.

Some of the zoos started breeding them to be able to cut down on the cost of the food supplies. What they didn't know at the time is these goats would become a huge attraction for visitors. People of all ages would ooh and aah at these miniature creatures. They were often displayed as part of petting areas for hands on enjoyment.

I for one was appalled when I found out why the Nigerian Dwarf goats were first introduced to the USA. They were offered as a food source for the large cats in captivity including lions and tigers. It is hard for me to think about these beloved creatures being a source of food.

On the bright side, it is my understanding that is no longer the case and they aren't being fed to larger animals. If that had never occurred we wouldn't be able to enjoy them so I guess everything does happen for a reason.

Many of the people who saw them in the zoo setting decided they wanted to have a few as pets or for breeding purposes. Quite a few people will tell you they would rather have goats than dogs as pets. Being able to enjoy them at the zoo though is one thing. Being responsible for them day after day is a huge responsibility so carefully think about it before you go shop for goats.

Size

A full grown Nigerian Dwarf goat male is known as a buck and the full grown females are referred to as a doe. They typically don't grow taller than 23 ½ inches/ .59 meters for males and 22 ½ inches/.57 meters for females.

The overall size is about 50 pounds/22 kilos for a male and 40pounds/18 kilos for a female. Of course they can vary from about 35 pounds/15 kilos to as much as 75 pounds/34 kilos. It depends on genetics, their diet, amount of exercise, location, and other variables.

The females produce about 1 quart of milk per day. However, the amount will vary based on the genetics, age, diet, and other factors. The milk is very rich and has a wonderful flavor. The milk is commonly used for various types of cheese production.

These goats offer a variety of colors. This includes a creamy white or tan color, shades of brown, and shades of black. They may be solid colors or have spotted areas. The Nigerian Dwarf goat is very durable and adaptable. They are able to survive in a variety of conditions including harsh environments when necessary.

Life Cycle

Breeding can occur for these goats at any time of the year. They will breed as long as they aren't experiencing high stress and their basic needs are being met. It takes between 145 and 155 days for gestation to occur. Females are sexually mature around 8 months old. For males it is about 3 months of age.

Females can give birth to up to 4 at a time, called kids. They each weigh about 2 pounds. With the right medical care and conditions, they can live up to 15 years.

Behaviors

Nigerian Dwarf goats can thrive in almost any environment. That is a plus when it comes to keeping them as pets, milk/cheese production, or for a profitable breeding business. They are very calm and quite playful. They make good companions for each other and for people. They do very well around children, adults, and the elderly.

Well Informed Decision

I absolutely love the Nigerian Dwarf goats. In fact, my children have been raising a few on their own. They selected them as projects for 4-H. Not all 4-H programs accept them but where we live they do. It has taught them responsibility, patience, and they love their goats. I plan to share with you everything it takes to properly care for these goats. I feel if you have the right information from the start, it helps you to make up your mind. If you have any hesitations about the time involved, the room for them, or the cost involved, please don't get them.

If you have a love of animals, you want something that doesn't take up very much space, and you enjoy these goats then they can be a wonderful addition to your household. I can't tell you the number of times just seeing our Nigerian Dwarf goats have put a smile on my face.

Pros

- Smaller than other goats

- Fun animals to have around
- They make great pets
- They interact well with each other and with humans
- They can be trained
- They offer milk
- Offspring can be sold
- Teach responsibility
- Reduce stress by interacting with them

Cons

- Startup costs for shelter and other necessities
- Daily commitment to feed them, clean up after them, and to interact with them
- Ongoing costs for feeding and caring for them
- Preventative care including vaccines, deworming, and hoof trimming
- Emergency medical care can be expensive
- They can be clever escape artists
- They can be noisy

Chapter 2 - Understanding the Nigerian Dwarf Goat

Understanding the Nigerian Dwarf goat can help you to decide if you would like to raise them. The more you know about their needs the easier it is for you to think about your willingness to commit to them or not. Sure, they are adorable but there is far more to owning them than just how they look.

For many people, their short statue is attractive. They want animals that are small enough to control and yet also produce milk for them. They may decide this is a better option for them than full size goats or cows due to the size. They need to socialize regularly with other goats and with you so don't get them if you don't have time to spend with them daily.

Height Standards

In the first chapter, I briefly covered the height standards. They typically don't grow taller than 23 ½ inches/ .59 meters for males and 22 ½ inches/.57 meters for females. However, they can also be further broken down. This is important to understand due to the organizations that represent these goats.

To make a comparison, think about a full grown adult Labrador. They are amazing dogs without a doubt. Average size is between 21 ½ inches/.55 meters and 23 ½ inches/.59 meters with the females being larger than the males. These dogs and Nigerian Dwarf goats are about the same height.

You don't have to go out there with a measuring stick to see how tall your goats are. If they are shorter/taller than average don't worry about it. Goats are just like people and they will have different sizes due to genetic markers and factors.

The American Goat Association and the American Dairy goat Association only acknowledge them as Nigerian Dwarf goats if they are less than 22 ½ inches/.57 meters for the females and 23 ½ inches/.59 meters for the males. However, the Nigerian Dwarf Goat Association classifies them at 17 to 19 inches/ .43 to .48 meters. Any goats over 23 inches/.58 meters aren't able to be registered with them.

Now, those statistics DO matter to you if you plan to breed your goats or if you plan to show them. We have one who is too tall for these regulations so my kids can't show him. However, he is and will always be one of our most amazing pets with a delightful personality that we adore.

If you plan to buy Nigerian Dwarf goats to breed or to show, ask the person selling them about the height of both parents. This information can help you to decide if you will make the purchase or not. Of course there are recessive gene factors so it isn't 100% foolproof but it can be a start.

Colors and Patterns

It is a common mistake that all Nigerian Dwarf goats are white in color. They can be. In some locations the majority of them are and that could be where this misinformation stems from. However, they are found with a variety of colors including white/cream, black, red, and gold.

There are quite a few patterns of colors that have been identified for the Nigerian Dwarf goats. The Buckskin pattern is very popular. This is present where the goat is brown with a cape of black over the head and around the neck region. The Chamoisee is often dark in color but with white on the ears. This white color is often referred to as frosting.

The Nigerian Dwarf Goat Association offers photos and explanations of the various patterns for the right terms. This information is helpful when you are registering your goats. Some

13

goats are easy due to being a solid color or they have a specific pattern.

If you aren't sure of the category for registering, don't worry. Send several photos along with your application and you can get help. You can also email photos and ask which category is best to place them in. Then you can finish your application and submit it.

Not all goats fit easily into a given category. There are those for goats with blue eyes and one for those with random patterns. Knowing the certain patterns though can help you identify what you want when you go shop for your goats.

Blue eyes are a dominant trait of Nigerian Dwarf goats. Yet only a small number of them actually have them. Breeders often look for this characteristic when it comes to which of the males and females they will allow to mate together. Their goal is often to get the best characteristics for the offspring.

These miniature goats are horned, but you often don't see them for sale that way. Many of the breeders will remove them, called disbudding, when they are about 2 weeks old. When you shop for baby goats, ask if they will remove the horns or if you need to do it. Don't assume it was done at an early age while they were still dependent on their mother.

If you plan to have the goats as pets you will need to decide to disbud them or not. I recommend you do as it makes it safer for the goats. They won't risk getting them tangled in fencing. They can't use the horns as a means of fighting over territory with other goats.

The more of them you have, the more import this is to think about as they will establish their own hierarchy among them. Removing the horns also makes it safer for people to be around the goats.

In a later section of this book, I do cover the process of disbudding the goats. It doesn't hurt them and it doesn't take too much time to complete the process. Yet knowing the right way to do it and feeling confident to do it is very important.

The older the young goats are the more difficult it is to remove the horns. As they get older, the horns will become secure to the bone of the skull. By doing it very early, around 2 weeks of age, that isn't a concern.

Show Goat Disqualifications

As I mentioned, my children have raised and shown Nigerian Dwarf goats as part of their school projects. If you plan to show your goats at these or other types of events, you need to make sure they won't be disqualified. Find out what the regulations are for that particular entity. Don't make the mistake of thinking they will be the same across the board.

Silver coloring is often not accepted for goat competitions. Therefore, you want to avoid those with such coloring if your goal is to raise them for competition purposes. If they are deemed to be overweight, they can also be disqualified. Keep a close eye on their diet and the amount of exercise they get.

Signs of Myotonia can also result in Nigerian Dwarf goats from being disqualified from various competitions. You may know that term more with fainting goats. They aren't a myth, some of them get so nervous they actually faint often around people! Such characteristics include:

- A Roman nose
- Ears which are pendulous
- A coat that curls
- Delayed relaxation around the eyes
- Rigid muscles
- Restricted motor skills

Experts believe Myotonia is the result of a genetic mutation. When possible, try to see the adults when you are contemplating buying baby goats. If they faint when you look at them you should avoid buying those particular offspring.

If you find later you have any goats with Myotonia, they can still be wonderful pets but they may faint on you at various times. They may do it quite often or just once in a while. My parents have one that only seems to faint when there are new people around.

There are some vets who recommend medication for Nigerian Dwarf goats who faint often. Others say it is just a genetic situation and the side effects of the medications are far worse than them actually fainting. They don't hurt themselves by fainting most of the time, but keep objects away from their living environment that could pose a threat.

Our vet has recommended any goats with Myotonia should be exercised more in order to give them better muscle tone. However, we haven't had a chance to do this as our goats we know don't faint. My mom tends to baby her one that does and they bond quite well.

Know the Guidelines

Since each type of program, show, or competition can have its own guidelines, I strongly encourage you to find out about them. If you already know the types of events you will take part in, make sure they are parallel with the types of goats you shop for and purchase.

Know the disqualifications for any event before you enter it. You don't want to show up and find out you can't participant. Most of the time, you won't get your entry fees back either. Just about every event has a list of qualifications for you to review. If you don't understand something, contact them to gain better insight.

Behaviors

Even though I love the look of these miniature goats, I enjoy taking care of them. They are very easy to care for and they can be trained without too much effort. They are quite intelligent and it still amazes me how much they can learn if you invest some time to spend with them.

They tend to bond very well with humans. However, that is only going to occur if you go out there and spend time with them on a consistent basis. If you're only out there to feed them they aren't going to bond with you. Sometimes, it is necessary to bottle feed some of the young. They will be clingy to humans so you have to make extra time for them.

My children have trained various Nigerian Dwarf goats to walk on a leash! That's right, and it was much easier than training a dog to walk correctly on a leash by all means. If you don't plan to breed your males, they should be neutered. This will increase their level of obedience. It also reduces the risk of you having far more of these goats to care for than you wanted.

Difference Between Nigerian Dwarf and Pygmy Goats

I would like to point out there are differences between Nigerian Dwarf and Pygmy goats. Too many people assume they are the same but they aren't! They are often mistaken though due to the similarities in size and behaviors. Both make excellent pets.

However, Pygmy goats are often raised for meat rather than for milk production. They are also more territorial and aggressive with each other than Nigerian Dwarfs. They are also harder to handle as they get older.

With that in mind, make sure the goats you buy for pets are actually Nigerian Dwarfs and not Pygmy goats. I have heard of people complaining about the demeanor of their goats, and I immediately think to myself they have the wrong breed and don't realize it.

Socialization

In chapter 1, I briefly mentioned the social desires of the Nigerian Dwarf goat. I can't stress to you enough that you shouldn't have just one of them. Even if you interact with them often, they will long for the socialization with their peers. You should have at least a pair of them if you plan to keep them happy and content.

When they are isolated, it is going to increase the risk of negative behavior developing. It can also result in them consistently being vocal. They may destroy their environment and try to get out of their fencing. They may not eat well and suffer from depression. I think we can all agree that isn't the way you want any animals in your care to survive.

They engage in a variety of behaviors for socialization. The young goats will often tumble and rough house with each other. They may get on the back of their mother and go for a ride! I have some great photos and videos of my goats having a good time.

They will interact with each other using a variety of sounds. Some of them are high pitched and others are deep. I think I spend enough time with my goats that I know some of what they are saying to each other. Yet there is still plenty that I am unaware of how to decipher it.

As you get to know your Nigerian Dwarf goats, you will be able to see how they respond and interact with each other. You will also be able to understand sounds from them that are distress related. Don't ignore those as it can mean your goat is sick or feels threatened. Do what you can to assess the situation and resolve the problem quickly.

They are exceptional mothers to their young, and teach them all they need to know. I love to watch the young kids with the doe because she is so in tune with her offspring. They are very patient, even with several little ones to care for at a time. They are proactive with their young and can easily identify their vocalizations from those of others.

I once had to move some of the older offspring further away from the fencing where their mother was. The two goats were moved after they were weaned. However, their mother could still identify their vocal sounds even though they had been separated for many months. It seemed to create anxiety for her.

Even though she had some new kids to care for, she was torn between her commitment to the new and to the older ones. The solution was for us to build additional fencing further away. It helped her to be calm and to focus on her young. However, it was a learning lesson for me that their commitment and their bonds are very strong.

Chapter 3 - Know the Law

Just because you love the idea of owning Nigerian Dwarf goats doesn't mean you legally can. The laws can be very different in the USA and the UK regarding ownership. They can be very different when it comes to areas within the USA or the UK too.

Part of the reason such regulations are in place is for the harmony of you and your neighbors. Goats of any kind, including Nigerian Dwarf goats, can be very noisy. You don't want your neighbors complaining that they can hear them at all hours. Think about how you would feel if the situation was reversed.

It is your responsibility to find out what the law is where you reside. You can't use the laws where you buy the goats. For example, if you buy them in one state but you live two states away the laws in your state are what you have to adhere to, not the laws for the location where you purchased your goats.

As a disclaimer, information about such ownership can change often. The laws and regulations can change based on problems and the solutions that are put into place. It is your responsibility to know the law before you buy Nigerian Dwarf goats. It is also your responsibility to stay current on any changes in the law after you buy them.

Stating you didn't know or you had the wrong information isn't going to help you out of the situation. This can result in you going to court. It can also result in a fine. Again, the penalties can vary from one location to the next.

Zoning

There may be certain areas where you can keep Nigerian Dwarf goats. For example, many locations don't allow them within city limits. However, you can live on the other side of that invisible line and own them without any problems at all. Find out what the zoning regulations are where you reside.

Number of Goats

There may be ordinances about the number of goats you can have on your property at any given point in time. Now, you have to find out about this based on where you live! Don't just drive around and say OK I saw a property where they had 10 so I know I can have at least 10!

What often happens is ordinances change over time. It may have once been 10 but now it is only 6. The reason that the other person gets to have 10 though is they were grandfathered in. This means they already had 10 at the time the ordinance changed. So they get to continue with the old rules. However, anyone after that point in time getting goats has to adhere to the new rules.

Rental Property

Read your rental agreement if you don't own your property. It likely has some type of clause in there about having pets. If you are allowed to have pets, you should still talk to your landlord. Most of them don't mind a dog or a cat but they may not be happy with goats.

One reason for this is the property may not be set up for the goats in terms of shelter and other needs. Since you don't own the property you aren't going to be able to modify it or add on at your leisure. If you are renting property in the country it may have room to accommodate your goats.

Since you always want to be on great terms with your landlord, don't make any assumptions. Talk to them and make sure they will be accepting of the Nigerian Dwarf goats living there. If they aren't you can't have them until you move to another location where they would be permitted.

Inspections

There are locations in the USA and the UK where you agree to inspections when you have goats and other types of animals on your property. The inspector can come out at any time to investigate the living conditions of the animals. They are going to check their overall appearance, food supplies, water, and ask for records about immunizations and other preventative care.

If you are taking care of your goats like you should, there is nothing to worry about with such an inspection. If there are issues the inspector will talk to you about them as well as how to make positive changes. They will do a recheck to make sure those changes have been successfully implemented in a timely manner.

Such inspections are done randomly based on the laws and zoning regulations in your area. They are done to ensure the animals have their needs met. Sometimes, inspections are conducted because someone has called in to report neglect or other issues with goats. The role of the inspector is to always make sure the well-being of the goats is met.

Insurance

Depending on where you live, your homeowners insurance may require you to add your goats and their structures to your policy. The coverage can be useful should you have any loss to your property. Other insurance you can take out through your vet for your goats is also something to think about.

Many vet offices work with 3rd parties to offer insurance for pets now. The coverage can help to reduce the amount of money you pay out of pocket when your goats need preventative care, checkups, medication, or emergency medical care. It is a good idea to check it out. We have such insurance and it is very reasonably priced.

Paperwork

Find out if there is any paperwork you must complete to legally own Nigerian Dwarf goats where you live. You may need to complete an application that is submitted for approval. You may need to provide documentation about the use of the goats and how many goats you will keep on your property.

There is usually a fee associated with the filing of such paperwork. The fee has to be paid at the time you submit the application or it won't be accepted. Make sure all paperwork is completed accurately. If there is missing information your request could be delayed or denied.

If you aren't sure what is being asked on the paperwork, ask someone in charge to explain it to you in further detail. If you are asked to provide any additional documentation after you submit the paperwork, get it in as soon as you can.

Ownership Verification

You may need to provide documentation that proves you are the legal owner of the goats. Sad but true, these wonderful animals are sometimes stolen and the sold for a profit or people steal them and keep them as pets. The requirement to provide ownership verification in some locations helps to reduce the risk.

Not being able to provide documentation of ownership when it is required can result in you not being allowed to keep the goats. You should never buy any goats without getting registration paperwork and a bill of sale.

Legal Issues and Resolutions

As is the case with any pets, there can be legal issues that arise. Keeping your Nigerian Dwarf goats in a secure location will eliminate the chance of most of them happening. If your goats get into the property of someone else and cause damage you can be held liable.

If you don't provide documentation when someone buys your goats or they feel you weren't honest with them you may have to go to court for a civil case. It can be hard to prove negligence which is why you need to keep very good records of any goats you sell. If they got their vaccines and other care from you but didn't do well with the new owner you can't be held liable as you showed reasonable care for them.

Always keep great documentation with your goats no matter if you are a buyer or a seller. There can even be legal issues between you and a vet. Maybe you feel they charged you too much and you aren't going to pay the bill. Maybe you agree you owe them but can't pay the cost so they turned the bill over to collections.

No matter which side of any legal issue you are on with your goats, get representation from an attorney who knows these animals and the laws where you live. Show up to all court proceedings and follow the advice of your attorney in regards to getting the situation successfully resolved.

Chapter 4 – Health Risks

Keeping your goats healthy is very important. Since they share close quarters, one with a health problem can quickly harm them all. Their deep bonds with each other can also be a situation when one of them is ill or dies. The others can become very sad. Their behaviors may change and they may not eat.

As their owner, it falls on your shoulders to provide them with the safest environment possible. It is also your responsibility to make sure they don't become ill. Sure, there are times you can't prevent it and you just have to deal with the care they require to get better.

However, almost all of the health risks Nigerian Dwarf goats experience can be significnalty reduced with the right types of care. If you neglect to provide the care for them it is on your shoulders. Don't cut corners on preventative care in order to save money.

The harsh reality is it can create very serious health problems for your goats. You don't want them to become ill and sickly. You don't want to see them down a long path of recovery. It is heartbreaking to see young goats born sickly and at a low birth weight. Death can be the outcome for goats that don't have the right care too due to illness.

If you don't take proper care of your goats, they WILL become ill. It isn't a matter of IF but WHEN. In some locations, you may be charged with neglect or endangerment if your goats become ill and the situation is one which you could have prevented.

You can bet your vet won't be too happy with you either if your goats are suffering due to neglect of care. Talk to your vet about what needs to be done and when. Get your goats on a great preventative schedule.

Our vet comes out to check on our goats when they are ill. Otherwise, we load them up and take them to town for their vaccines and checkups. It isn't hard to get them there but you do need to make sure you have a trailer designed for them and that will safely haul them to and from the vet.

Prevention

I can't stress enough how important it is to understand the ongoing medical needs of your Nigerian Dwarf goats. It makes me very angry when owners seem to ignore this part of their overall care. If you aren't willing to commit to it then don't have them for pets.

Prevention is the best way you can care for your goats. It will reduce the risk of serious health problems developing. It will also keep them happier and extend their lifespan. Of course it is about the quality of those years and not the number of them.

Keep a record file for each of your goats so it is easy to find out what they need and when. Take notes and include the dates for when they are sick and what the problem was as well as the solution. Here are the items I keep on file for each of my goats:

- Dates of any illnesses
- Symptoms of any illnesses
- Duration of any illnesses
- Care for any illnesses
- Medications taken and when
- Vet appointments and visits
- Vaccinations
- Deworming

Vaccines

The good news is there are very few diseases you need to worry about when it comes to these goats. The fact that most of them have vaccines to protect against them is also important. Failure to follow through with them means your goats are very vulnerable.

Your goats need to be immunized each year with C&D Tetanus and Rabies. They also need to get a Selenium injection. You can get the supplies and complete the injections on your own. I prefer to allow my vet to take care of it for us.

If you decide to do the injections on your own, make sure you know the procedure before you do so. Giving the injections wrong can put your goats at risk. Never use the same needle on more than one goat. Use safety precautions and dispose of sharp ends in a medically approved container.

When my container is full, I take it to our local health department. That is the only place I know of where you can dispose of the sharp needle ends from vaccines or antibiotics. Don't toss them in the trash because that can put people and animals at risk that may come into contact with them.

Antibiotics

Our vet has given us a small supply of antibiotics that we keep on hand. We have had Nigerian Dwarf goats long enough that we feel comfortable doing this. However, not everyone has the right training so don't be offended if your vet refuses.

Don't buy antibiotics for your goats from the black market. You can buy what you want online, but you have no way to know who you are really buying them from. You don't know the quality of them either. Stick with getting them from your vet.

Just like humans, goats can build up a tolerance to antibiotics so they should be used only for certain bacterial infections. They won't work for a virus. When your goat needs them, the dose should be given daily for the duration. This can be 3, 5, 7, or 10 days depending on the product. If you stop giving them the medication early the infection can start all over again.

While none of our goats have had an allergic reaction to antibiotics or other medications, it can happen. Watch your goats the first time you give them such a product. If they show any signs of acting differently or they appear swollen or disoriented you need to call your vet immediately.

Pneumonia

Sadly, we have lost a few of our goats to pneumonia. I didn't realize the spring and summer months are when it is the most common. I tend to assume such health problems would be more prominent during the cold weather months. However, it can be harmful or deadly all year long.

Watch your goats closely for any signs of pneumonia. These signs can include:

- Nasal discharge (yellow in color)
- Labored breathing
- High temperature (taken rectally)

Goats can go from being fine to very sick to dying in 24 hours or less when they have pneumonia. Don't mess around with it; call your vet immediately if you have any concerns. Antibiotics can be administered for several days to help them recover but you have to act quickly.

Worms

It is important to keep the living quarters for the goats clean. If not, the feces left there can get into their water and where they are grazing for food. The result of this can be worms. Cleaning up often will reduce this from happening. Make sure the water buckets are cleaned out from time to time to kill any germs and bacteria.

It is a good idea to alternate the areas where the Nigerian Dwarf goats can graze. This gives you an opportunity to clean up the feces in a given area while they graze in another location. You can take samples of feces to your vet and they can test the pellets to let you know if worms are present.

If so, they can help you with creating a plan of action to kill the worms. At the same time you will need to work on improving the clean up so the problem doesn't continue to manifest for your goats.

I highly recommend you save yourself the trouble of fighting worms. You can protect against them from the start. I do this every 3 months and I have never had to deal with worms with my Nigerian Dwarf goats. This isn't a free pass though to not clean their living quarters though!

I recommend products such as Eprinex because it works for both external and internal worm control. It is easy to administer and you don't have to withdraw from milking them for any period of time.

Worms affecting your Nigerian Dwarf goats can become immune to deworming products over time. With that in mind, don't use the same product for more than a year. Here are some of the products I have used over the years on our goats to keep worms at bay:

- Equimectrin
- Ivomec
- Panacur
- Safeguard
- Valbazen (NEVER give this to any goats who are confirmed or possibly pregnant)
- Zimecterin

Following the dosing instructions for the specific deworming product you have is important. If you don't give your goats the right amount, they can still get worms. If you give them too much there is the risk of serious side effects. Since many of these

29

products aren't specifically labeled with doses for goats, talk to your vet to verify the dose before you administer it.

There are some herbal deworming products on the market. I know several people who have tried them and then their goats still got worms. I have never used such products so I can't give you my own take on it.

Even when you take preventative action to prevent worms, your goats may still get them. Check their feces every couple of weeks as you clean up. This will be a telling sign of any problems. Of course if you have changed their diet then that can account for feces changes too.

When you haven't changed their diet, stools that are mushy may be a sign there is a parasite issue among your goats. That is a good time to contact your vet to check some stool samples for you. They can confirm or rule out the presence of parasites. If they are confirmed, they can help you customize a plan of action to eliminate them.

Lice

The longer the hair is on the goats, the greater the risk is of them getting lice. Once one of your goats has it, expect them all to. Lice can spread very quickly as these ugly creatures can jump from one of them to the next. Since goats are highly social, they are in close proximity to each other all the time.

Brushing your goats often will help to reduce the risk of lice. However, it is a myth that only dirty goats will get lice. It can develop in very clean ones as well. If you do discover lice, you need to combat it quickly. Talk to your vet about safe products to use. You may need to use different products if you rely on the goats for milk production. Females who are pregnant may need special formulas as well.

Mastitis

This is a type of infection that can develop around the udders for the female goats who are lactating. The openings to the teats don't close after milking. It doesn't matter if it is due to nursing the young or the goat being milked by a human.

If the doe lies down in a bedding area or grass area that is wet, bacteria could be present. This can get into her body through the teat openings. Do your best to keep the housing areas very clean to prevent this from occurring.

Calculi

Males can develop problems with kidneys that lead to urinary tract stones. This is going to be an issue if you feed your goats a diet that is high in calcium. If they are making odd sounds or appear to be in pain, they may have such an infection. Urinating very frequently is also a sign of infection.

You may have to contact your vet to get them antibiotics to clear up the infection. Make sure you complete the entire course of the medication. Otherwise, the infection can flare up again and you will have to start treatment all over again.

Hooves

I will admit, I don't like the process of trimming the hooves of our Nigerian Dwarf goats. Yet you can't pass this important need or they can develop a limp and become lame. Their hooves grow all the time so you need to pay attention. Different seasons influence growth with the summer being the fastest.

Not all of the goats will have hooves that grow at the same speed. I keep a chart so I know when I clipped for a given goat. I recommend doing this because it can be very easy to lose track.

I have found the best way to do the hooves is with a pair of pruning shears, but they must be sharp! You can also buy a specific trimming tool but the shears work well and cut out another expense. Carefully snip the bottom of each hoof until it is parallel to the growth rings. Take your time so you don't cut them too short.

Always sanitize your shears before you use them on any goat. If they get dull take the time to sharpen them. Clean them again before you use them on another goat. If there is a fungus or other type of problem with one of the goats, you certainly don't want to risk spreading it to others because the shears were dirty. Take the time to clean them when you are done too. It may seem redundant but taking precautions significantly reduce the risk of health problems for your goats.

Mold

Make sure you keep your hay free from mold. Goats are very susceptible to the toxins mold can offer. Never allow them to eat food that has mold on it as it will make them ill or kill them. Even breathing in the toxins from mold around their living quarters can be harmful to them.

Mold can develop if you leave food sources out where the goats can soil in it and walk through it. All food sources should be placed where they can't get them. I have the hay in a separate pen close to their living quarters. It is easy for me to access it but I don't have to worry about them causing bacteria or mold development.

Environmental Poisons

You would never leave any type of poison out where your household pets or your children could get them. Therefore, it goes without reason that you can't leave such products where your goats can get them either. Remember, they are very curious by nature and they can climb just about anything.

Make sure you don't have any forms of poisonous weeds or plants around your land where the goats will be able to explore and eat. If you aren't sure, it is a good idea to have them tested before you even consider buying any Nigerian Dwarf goats. Exposure to such poisons can make them quite ill or kill them.

Some of the plants and weeds that can make your goats sick or kill them you would never think about. They include the following, but keep in mind this isn't a complete list. It is up to you to identify what is accessible to them where you live and how safe or unsafe it is for them.

- Azalea
- Cherry
- Laurel
- Rhododendron
- Yew

Vet

Find a wonderful vet in your area with the skills and desire to care for Nigerian Dwarf goats. We were lucky enough that the vet we have used for our dogs is also able to offer us care for our goats. Any time your goat doesn't seem to be eating or behaving normally you should call your vet.

You should feel able to freely communicate with your vet and ask any questions. They should have an emergency number you can call any time of the day or night. It is important to be able to get help from your vet if you have a serious Nigerian Dwarf goat issue outside of office hours.

Some of the health problems they encountered develop very quickly. Waiting a few days or even until morning could prove to be too late to help them. Don't feel guilty about calling your vet at night or on the weekends if you believe something just isn't right with any of your goats.

Healthy Goats

Any time you plan to add new goats to your herd, make sure they are healthy. Don't make the mistake of bringing home one that has lice, worms, or other health problems. Many of the issues including TB, Brucellosis, and CAE can be contagious and spread to the rest of your goats before you have any idea what is taking place.

With this in mind, some people only get new goats when those they own have offspring. They know the care they have been given and they aren't going to bring in anything detrimental to the herd.

Healthy goats are very content as well as alert. They have a good appetite and they chew cud. The coat is glossy and smooth. While the ribs can be felt under the skin, they aren't sticking out. Their pellets are moist rather than dry and they aren't runny. Watch your goats when they urinate too as it shouldn't appear to be difficult or painful.

The normal body temperature of Nigerian Dwarf goats is between 101 and 103 F. The normal pulse is between 70 and 80 beats per minute. Don't be alarmed if your goats are a bit off this scale. They are offered as target points for evaluation. Each of them will have different variables that influence these factors. For example, a goat that is excited or nervous will have a much higher pulse than normal.

I keep several supplies on hand to help me care for my goats well. I suggest putting together a kit with such items for you to be able to easily access. Here is what I have in mine:

- Rubber gloves
- Emergency vet numbers
- Thermometers (ear model and rectal model)
- Hoof trimmers
- Deworming medication

- Probios (healthy bacteria medication)
- Wound Coat (topical ointment for cuts, scrapes, and to apply after disbudding)
- Lice dust
- Pepto Bismol (for diarrhea to prevent dehydration)
- Syringes
- Needles
- Antibiotics (Bio-Mycin and Penicillin)
- CD&T vaccinations

Chapter 5 - Housing

Your Nigerian Dwarf goats are going to need a secure place to live. Since I am on a farm, I have room to provide them with shelter that isn't too close to my house. My wife loves the goats but not the sound of them socializing at all hours! She wants it quiet when she sleeps.

I know people who keep their goats in their backyard. They live in an area where it is acceptable to have them as pets. I don't recommend keeping them in your house as you would a dog or a cat. Goats need plenty of space to roam so being confined indoors can make them very stressed.

Before you go shopping for goats, you need to think about where you will house them. You also need to think about how many goats you can realistically house in that given area. Don't be tempted when you go shopping to take home 6 when you really only have room for 4!

Their housing should provide them with the following:

- Space to move around freely and explore
- Proper ventilation
- Shelter from the elements
- Protection from predators
- Fencing to provide boundaries
- Secure feeling
- Sleeping Quarters
- Areas to Eliminate waste from the body

Space

Your goats need plenty of space to graze around. This can be a pasture or it can be an enclosed area that has hay in it. Don't limit them too much because they will have too much energy and no

36

way to burn it off. They should be able to move freely and never be in an isolated area unless they are sick or giving birth.

One of my pet peeves with some breeding set ups is the goats have very little room. They can barely turn around in the cages they are kept in. When you have Nigerian Dwarf goats as pets you need to give them ample room for security and for roaming.

If you allow them to access a pasture, it needs to be free from any risks. This includes plants and weeds that could be harmful or deadly to your goats. As mentioned in a previous chapter, it is your responsibility to carefully identify what you have in place where your goats will reside.

Fencing

Your fencing needs to be secure. It should have small openings so your goats can't get out. If the openings in the fence are too wide, they can use them as foot holds and get over the top. If you have wide fencing you can secure it by wrapping chicken wire around it on the outside.

They are very intelligent and they will find ways to climb over and under fencing that isn't well installed. Check your fencing regularly for any loose areas that need to be repaired. It doesn't take much time to walk around the parameter of it and check it now and then. Keep fencing supplies on hand too. Then you can fix any problems as soon as you identify them.

Your goats could get their body parts stuck in fencing that is too wide so don't provide them with such an opportunity. Their heads and hoofs are often parts that they can get out but not the rest of the body. Be mindful of the kids as they can squeeze through small openings and their mother won't be able to follow them. It is really amazing how they can manipulate what you think is secure.

With that in mind, watch them carefully when you first get your goats. If you notice they are accessing any areas, secure them more. Don't just assume it is all good and then you have to go searching for your goats. They can end up accessing entities that make them sick or kill them.

They can get out there into roads or become prey for other animals in the area. You will be very heartbroken if such an outcome occurs because you didn't secure the fencing well enough for your goats. It is going to be a learning experience but knowing how important this is will hopefully help you to really put some thought into what you offer to keep them in a given place.

Fencing needs to be high enough that the goats can't climb over it. Never stack hay or other items in areas where they could climb it and then leap over the fencing. When Nigerian Dwarf goats escape it can be very difficult to find them. This also increases the risk of them coming into contact with something that can be harmful or fatal.

The fencing must be sturdy and it should be at least 4 feet high and 16 feet long. I recommend you use graduated livestock panels. They offer wrapped corners and they will hold up well.

This also ensures you don't have sharp edges which could result in scrapes or cuts on your goats.

We have several gates in our fencing area. I have done this to help keep certain goats separated at times. For example, there are times when I don't want the males to be where the females are because we aren't a breeding business.

Yet I don't want to have all of our males nurtured as there are times we will breed a pair. I also have gates in place so I can segregate a goat or two if they don't feel well or for a youngster and its mother should it need some extra rest and care.

It isn't hard or expensive to place several gates along the areas where you keep your Nigerian Dwarf goats. By doing so, you give yourself plenty of space to work and to take care of their needs quickly. You will appreciate these gates when you are cleaning up too.

Just clean up one area and then move the goats into that location while you work on cleaning up the rest. Otherwise, you will find they continually bother you while you are trying to clean up after them. They may think you are there to play with them and they get in the way.

Ventilation

Ensure the enclosure for your goats has proper ventilation. There should be air circulating so the area doesn't get too hot or too cold. You may need to offer different types of set ups at various seasons. It depends on the changes in the temperatures where you reside.

If they aren't comfortable in their living conditions they won't thrive. The good news is these goats are able to do well in a variety of climates and temperatures. Even so, it is your responsibility to make sure they have a secure location that keeps them as comfortable as possible no matter what time of year it happens to be.

Shelter from the Elements

Make sure your location for the goats offers some shelter from the elements. We have an enclosure with an open side to it. This allows the goats to decide if they want to spend time in the sunlight or in the shade. It also gives them an area to explore without getting into trouble.

Studies show heat stress can reduce milk production, reproduction, and eating habits for these goats. It can also result in them being more aggressive towards each other. If you live in an area where it gets very hot during the summer you need to do all you can for your goats. You can offer them shaded areas, consider fans, and other resources for them.

There are quite a few shelter options you can consider. For example, a barn or shed can be modified to offer them a place to be away from the cold or the wind. If you only have a pair of Nigerian Dwarf goats you can even get by with a large sized dog house.

As a word of caution, be very careful what you make the shelter from! We put a metal roof on at first. Well, let's just say it scared the hell out of our sweet goats the first time it rained hard!

Goats don't like to be wet either. When it is raining or snowing they will all be trying to find shelter. Make sure the enclosure you offer has room for all of them to get out of the elements so they don't stress or become aggressive with each other.

Again, think about the climate where you live. If it hardly ever rains then it isn't as big of an issue. I live in an area where it can be a monsoon during certain times of the year with heavy rain storms to think about.

Sleeping Areas

Goats take up more space when they lie down than when they are awake. Keep that in mind as you need to give them ample space for stretching out and sleeping. Due to the social nature of goats, you will find they often sleep in close proximity to each other. However, if they don't have enough room they won't get the rest they really need.

Waste Areas

If your shelter area is large enough the goats will find a location where they pee and poop. This is important because you don't want them to have to do this business in the same area where they eat and drink. When waste can't be separated the risk of health problems is significantly increased.

Protect from Predators

We live out on a farm, and the risk of predators is very real to us. We have our Nigerian Dwarf goats well protected so they can't get out and predators can't get in. No matter where you live, it is a good idea to have such a design in mind. Remember, these goats can make a great meal for a larger predator. You certainly don't want to go out to tend to them and find such a gruesome outcome.

By nature, dogs and coyotes seem to be the greatest predators for you to worry about. However, I have had some close calls with mountain lions and foxes over the years. If your enclosure is good enough though it will keep your goats in and those predators at bay.

Food and Water

The housing area for your goats needs to provide them with safe access to food and water. We will cover their dietary needs in a future chapter. However, you need to make sure the food isn't going to be hard for them to access. They need to have access to fresh water at any time they desire it.

They tend to eat more food during the colder temperatures. They also tend to drink more water during the warmer times of the year. It is important to keep these changes in mind so you can adjust feeding and watering routines to fit their needs.

It isn't enough to have water for the goats in place though. It has to be clean water or they will refuse to drink it. They may be getting sick from not enough water but they aren't going to drink water that is dirty or smells bad.

Adding a few caps full of apple cider vinegar to water can make it drinkable for your goats. This is a great option instead of tossing out water they didn't drink. In the winter, you can add some molasses to the water to make it a bit sweeter.

We will talk much more about feeding and watering your goats in a future chapter. It is one of the key components to taking care of your goats successfully. The right balance of food ensures they are at a healthy weight and they have the nutritional value to grow as they should.

Chapter 6 – Exercise

Nigerian Dwarf Goats are social and playful. Use that to your advantage when it comes to getting them to exercise. Goats are creatures of habit so if you keep them active from the time you get them they will remain quite active. This will help them maintain a healthy weight and to keep their muscles flexible.

Goats that don't get enough exercise tend to suffer from boredom. This is when they can start to have negative behaviors with each other and with you. It can also result in health problems due to increased weight.

I enjoy going into the enclosure and playing with them. I also love my kids going outside to play with the goats. It is great exercise for all of us. If you live in town, you can take your goats out on a dog leash. We don't sit around the house doing nothing when we know we can get out and enjoy time with our goats.

Even at the times of year when it is colder out, we go out with them. We put on layers of clothing and bundle up. When it is the hot time of the year we go out early in the morning and then again at night when it cools off. Remember, if you have Nigerian Dwarf goats they are your responsibility all the time.

There is no room for excuses such as it is too hot or too cold. You can't say you are too busy or you just don't feel like getting out there with them to make sure they exercise. Don't assume they are getting enough of it on their own either. I know I do all I can to get them moving.

My kids also leash them up and train them so they can follow the commands for the competitions. It really depends on what your objectives are about what type of training you do with them. Lazy goats become fat goats and very vulnerable to serious health problems.

It is your responsibility as an owner to make sure every single goat is getting daily exercise. There are exceptions of course. When any of our goats are under the weather we give them time to rest rather than exercising. When females are ready to give birth or they have recently given birth we also allow them more resting time.

When your goats are rebounding from illness, you want them to be calm and to relax as much as possible. Pay attention to them and their energy level. If they seem to be ready for some mild exercise then take that lead. Take them out for a walk or let them out of a secure area and see what they do in terms of exploring.

The same is true with a female when she is pregnant. She may spend more time lying down and that is fine. As the birth gets closer she may start to find an area in the shelter where she can give birth and be comfortable as well as feel secure. Yet she may have days when she wants to get up and about and exercise.

The message I am trying to send overall is that your goats need plenty of exercise. Both through their daily playing and moving around and what you initiate with them. However, you shouldn't force it if they have health problems or a pregnancy. Goats tend to have less energy as they get older too so keep that in mind as they get up there in age.

Be Aware

Exercising your goats is fun, and it is more like play than work. In fact, I often do it to get out of the household chores! Don't tell my wife that though! I have learned the hard way some forms of play cause me trouble later on. For example, rubbing the head of a goat isn't a good idea. They will think it is a butting game and then they will butt you when they are bigger and when you aren't prepared for them to.

If you rub their chest or their neck, be aware of the location of other body parts. You don't want to accidentally get kicked or stepped on. They may be small but they can still be powerful enough for it to cause some pain. Be well aware of the messages you send your goats through interacting with them and you will be fine!

Climbing and Jumping

It is natural instinct for these goats to climb and jump. Don't hinder that for them. Some owners of Nigerian Dwarf goats do this because they don't want them to get hurt. Yet you have to find a balance and let them do what they are instinctively going to be programmed to do.

Offer them a safe area where they can do so. You can create it with a variety of items for a low cost. Just make sure it isn't around the fencing edges or they will escape. I love watching our goats as they climb, jump, and play. It is such a great form of entertainment!

It may sound silly, but I know people who have trampolines for their goats to jump on! They have dug a hole and placed the majority of the length of the legs of the trampoline down in there. Then the goats can climb on it and bounce but not be too far off the ground when they jump.

I haven't tried it but I have seen it in action and it does work. It is a personal choice about what you would like to offer to them. Make sure they can't climb areas where you have feed stacked and get over fencing. Make sure they can't climb anything which could potentially fall over and injure or kill your goats.

Interactions with Each Other

Nigerian Dwarf goats thrive on socializing with each other. I have mentioned several times that you must have at least 2 of them as one will be very sad and lonely. They will play with each other, stand close to each other, and vocalize to communicate with each other.

Personally, I think 4 is a great number. Not an excessive amount of work but more than enough! They don't get tired of interacting just with each other which can happen if you only have 2. My wife said from the beginning we must have an even number of goats so no one gets left out!

I don't know if that would happen, but we have always had the even number. At times, we have had up to 8 goats. This is due to the birth of little ones but we often sell them when they are weaned. There have been a few instances though when we have kept a baby goat to maturity.

For the most part, they aren't territorial and they will get along well. There is a type of hierarchy though that your herd will create internally. If they don't have enough space, enough exercise, or enough food and water though they will become very agitated with each other.

Experts believe this is due to their survival instincts. They know they have to do all they can to stay alive. Even if it means fighting another goat for shelter or taking food supplies and leaving other goats with none.

If you have too many males they may try to bump at each other and show who is stronger. Neutered males are the most relaxed and calm. However, I only recommend doing that if you don't plan to breed them with any of your females.

The females tend to get along well but they are quite protective of their offspring. They can change significantly in terms of being territorial when it comes to their young. They will do all they can to ensure their survival. This includes fighting for food if they need to. Instinctively, they know if they don't get enough food to eat they can't produce enough milk for their young to survive.

The females will also fight for a safe location within the shelter for her young to rest, to play, and to feed. The other goats tend to realize this and won't get in her way. I am quite amazed at how determined they can be when it comes to their young.

The younger goats are fun to watch. They jump, climb, even get on their mother's back for a ride. They are curious and they seem to have a never ending supply of energy. Their interactions with each other teach them how to survive and also how to be good parents themselves.

Types of Exercise

Most of the time your goats will engage in daily activities that provide them enough exercise. This includes exploring and playing. However, you need to observe them and monitor them. When kept as pets, you should take them for walks. You can do so with a leash and give them simple commands to follow.

If the goats will be shown such as for a 4-H project, they definitely need to get used to being on a leash. Your child will have to take them into the arena and walk them around. If the goat is out of control and dragging your kid along or your kid can't get the goat to walk then they won't do well in the competition.

Frequency

Exercise needs to take place daily for your goats. There are some exceptions though including when females are about to give birth and when one is sick. Give the pregnant females time to relax and to rest for the upcoming young they will be taking care of.

When a goat is sick, they may need plenty of rest in order for them to make a speedy recovery. Depending on their illness, they may need to be secluded from the rest of the herd for a short period of time.

For healthy Nigerian Dwarf goats, they should take part in some type of exercise on a daily basis. Try to incorporate this early on so it will be part of their daily habits. By nature, these creatures are quite active so it usually isn't a problem. However, if their living quarters are too limited that can hinder the ability for them to get sufficient exercise each day.

Consequences of Not Exercising Them

When your goats don't get enough exercise, they can put on extra pounds. This makes it harder for them to get around. It can also increase their risk of developing serious health problems. A lack of exercise can change their temperament and make them more aggressive.

Sometimes, goats who lack exercise due to limited environment may engage in behaviors that are destructive. They tend to tear up what they can get access to and that isn't going to make you very happy. Not enough exercise can shorten the years of a goat and also reduce the level of contentment they experience.

Not enough exercise can reduce mating efforts and thus result in fewer offspring. It can also reduce the overall health of the young due to a lower birth weight. This makes them more susceptible to mortality and to health problems.

Chapter 7 - Training

Goats are quite curious, and it is fine to allow them to explore. However, they also need to know limits that you have set. Otherwise, they can get hurt, they can be out of control, and they can develop aggressive habits. Ideally, you should start training when the goats are just a few months old.

Think about your kids for a moment – your human kids! From a young age you teach them the behaviors you find acceptable and those you don't. This is important so they grow up to be adults with limits and boundaries as well as being well rounded. The same is true of your young goats.

Some people tend to forget just how curious Nigerian Dwarf goats can be. They have very good memories and they learn quickly. They also can problem solve and find a variety of ways to get what they want. This is why you always have to think a few steps ahead of them to keep them safe.

When you have baby goats to work with, you can train them and teach them what you would like them to engage in. You can teach them behaviors you find appealing and you can help them to stop taking part in behaviors you don't.

This is the downside to buying a junior goat or a full grown adult who is amateur. They are already set in their ways. They can still be trained but it is going to be far more difficult to get them to follow the commands. Know what you are getting involved in from the start and be patient with them.

Positive Reinforcement

Never yell, hit, or withhold affection from your goats due to behaviors. You need to teach them through positive reinforcement. By praising them for doing what you like they will be stimulated to continue to repeat such behaviors. By yelling or hitting them you are only going to upset them. Such actions can make them anxious and aggressive.

Why Train them?

You would never think to let your children or your other household pets to do as they pleased. This can quickly get out of control and it can result in both damages and in them getting hurt. This is the biggest reason why you need to train your Nigerian Dwarf goats. They need to be able to explore but not have complete freedom.

When you keep them as pets, you need to fully enjoy them. Goats that aren't well trained will test your patience. They will engage in behaviors that make you crazy on a regular basis. Finally, you will make the decision to get rid of them. I have seen that happen and it isn't good for anyone involved.

When it has happened, they asked me why my goats didn't do this or do that. They told me I must have an unreal amount of patience. I explained it had nothing to do with that but with the training for my goats. Sometimes, I have been able to find out about the issue early enough to intervene but more often than not they have already gotten rid of the goats.

Types of Training

The types of training you provide to your goats depends on what you want them to do. Sometimes, it is just a simple command with your voice that gets them to do a particular task. Other times, it is when you open a section of the gates they will know to enter at that time. If you plan to walk your goats then you need to train them to follow a lead on a leash.

Some methods of training are super easy, so don't make it complicated. I have had a few goats that chew on everything. This included my daughter's long blonde hair. Blowing in their face is all it takes to make them stop. After several cause and effect incidents of this taking place they stopped doing it.

Use Collars

Get your young goats used to wearing a collar. This helps you with training them and guiding them. The collar can be used with a leash when you need to load up your goats for a visit to the vet. You can use collars and a leash to hold your goats still while you milk them, brush them, and take care of their hooves.

Over time, they will come to understand what the procedure is going to be. My adult goats stand there for me to milk them. They stand there for me to brush them and to click their hooves. Each time we have young ones to work with we go back to the collar and leash scenario. It is one of the simplest and cost effective methods of training your goats you will find.

Make sure the collar fits securely but not too tight. Your goat should be able to move its neck freely. However, if the collar is too loose they will be able to slip right out of it. You should be able to put your finger between the collar and their coat.

I use retractable leashes for your Nigerian Dwarf goats. I do this because there are times when we are just going for a stroll to exercise and I give them more slack so they can explore. Yet I can retract and keep the goat very close to me if they are skittish or they are sick.

Handle them Often

The difference between goats as wonderful pets and wild goats is the amount of handling they get from humans. If you don't interact with them often they are going to be wild. They will run from you and they will struggle to get away from you when you attempt to put a collar on them. This makes grooming them, milking them, and transporting them very difficult.

As your goats get used to you handling them, they are going to come to you when you walk out to the area. You can even call their names and they will come see what you are doing. Teach your goats from an early age that you will be handling and how you expect them to act with that process.

A common mistake I often see is someone allowing a goat to keep their head down when they handle them. Ducking the head is an instinctive element for them to get away from someone or something. Gently but firmly place your hand under the chin of the goat and they will hold their head up. Don't jerk upward on the leash attached to the collar as that will choke the goat.

Be in Control

Never chase any goat. Teach them you are in control and encourage them to come to you. At first you will need to be very patient. You can coax them with your voice and with treats. Peanuts, apples, and carrots are treats they often can't resist! Pet them when they come to you and talk to them. They need to know they are safe when they interact with you.

As they start to come to you faster, cut down on the sweets you offer them. You should still give them plenty of praise and pet them and rub their bellies. Show them affection each time they come to you as a means of strengthening your bond with them.

On a side note, if one of your goats does run away from you, grab the back leg to catch it. If you grab the goat by a front leg you may cause a fracture or break. If you are good at roping, you can also tie their back legs or rope around their neck to get them to stop running.

Teach them Manners

People often laugh at me when I tell them I teach my Nigerian Dwarf goats manners. I certainly don't want to deal with bad behavior from them day after day. I teach them manners and I also teach my own children manners and it keeps life happy for all of us!

When goats don't follow manners, it can cause injury to them, other goats, or to you. Nothing is going to ruin your idea of enjoying these goats as them being out of control. When goats misbehave, it isn't because they are trying to ruin your day so don't take it personal. However, you can't just dismiss those behaviors either as they will only get worse.

Sometimes, the reason a goat takes part in bad behavior is due to your actions. For example, don't push down on the head of a goat. When you do so, their natural instinct is to butt with you. The last thing you want is your goats to think butting you and other humans is acceptable behavior. Even though your goats may be excited to see you, don't allow them to jump on you. This can be dangerous and the older they get the more of a risk it becomes. Command DOWN in a loud voice and firmly push them off of you. This should break the behavior quickly. Don't let them push their two front legs on you either. This can be dangerous for their spine and it can risk injury to their legs.

I hope it goes without saying, but goats aren't for riding. If your kids want to ride you need to get them a pony. Goats tend to become very afraid when there is a person on their back. This can result in them running and getting hurt as well as hurting the child. There is also the risk of back pain or a broken back.

Getting Started

Don't feel overwhelmed when it comes to training your goats. Since we had these goats growing up, I have always been around them. However, as an adult I realized my parents didn't give them much training. My kids do because of the rules and regulations they must follow for 4-H competitions. To help you keep it all under control, make a list of what you would like to train your goats to do.

Once you have your list, prioritize it. What is the first thing they need to learn? What is the second? Introduce those two objectives daily until they get them right. Don't add any more tasks for training until they have mastered the first two. Continue to move down your list in order of priority.

Keep in mind some of the training tasks will be easy and accomplished in very little time. Others are going to take a tremendous amount of time and energy. You need to be able to see ongoing progress but don't rush the training. You don't want you or the goats to experience stress.

Consistency

Part of your plan of action needs to include being consistent. Nigerian Dwarf goats are very intelligent. However, if you don't train them consistently you will confuse them. You need to offer them the same experience or the same words for the given result you want each time. Try to practice training your goats on a daily basis. Even if you are only about do so for 30 minutes per day it is better than nothing. If you can't commit to everyday then you need to be able to commit to every other day. If there is too much time between training sessions, your goats will regress instead of moving forward with their learning.

Keep in mind their attention span isn't going to allow you to train them for more than 30 minutes at a time. You may have to do less than that with younger goats and then add time as they get older. You can't try to cram all of your training into a 2 hour session on Saturday as your goats will lose interest long before that time ends.

Challenges

When you have several Nigerian Dwarf goats, you will find that they respond differently to the training. This can make it hard to keep moving forward when there is a gap in their learning and behaviors. You may have to engage in one on one training sessions to get the most from them.

Time can be a challenge because we all have so much on our plates. However, you just have to carve out the time to get the training completed. The more you engage in it the more it will just become part of the daily routine.

External factors can hinder the training too. This can include changes in climate, the temperament of the goats, eating and drinking habits, and any illnesses. Do your best to reduce the external factors that can become barriers to successful training.

Rewards

To keep your goats engaged in the training, give them verbal encouragement and praise. They will respond well to your voice. Pat them on the head and rub them. They will enjoy such types of encouragement as a reward. You can also offer them slices of apples or pieces of carrots as an incentive. Never yell at your goats or withhold their basic needs when they don't follow your directions for training as planned.

Don't forget to reward yourself too for your efforts with the training. Think about something you really want and get it when you have consistently given it your all day after day to train your goats. If you are dedicated to it, you will notice improvements with them at regular intervals.

This is going to make your time with your Nigerian Dwarf goats far more enjoyable. It is also going to make them easier to care for. The time you invest in training pays off for the long term so keep that in mind when you get discouraged.

Chapter 8 - Feeding

Feeding your Nigerian Dwarf goats enough food but not too much is very important. For many potential owners, this can be an intimidating objective. Don't worry because when you are done reading this chapter of the book you will have plenty of information to help you obtain a positive outcome.

First of all, I would like to point out that by nature they are browsers. They can spend large chunks of time each day nibbling on trees and woody shrubs. They will eat the weedy areas too that other forms of livestock won't eat. This can cause them to eat too much and it can also result in them eating what they shouldn't. It is up to you to limit such scenarios.

I remember growing up on the farm my dad would let our goats go into the same pasture as the cows. There was plenty of food for both of them this way and it helped him to keep the conditions of the pastures improving. The cows would only eat the grass down to a certain point then it would just remain.

By putting out goats out there though, they would consume it to the bottom. This was a winning outcome that my dad was looking for. However, he had to be careful not to allow them to graze too long in one area. Otherwise, they would eat the grass down too far. Then it was almost impossible to get it to grow again.

You don't have to live on a farm though to allow your Nigerian Dwarf goats enough to eat. You just have to survey your circumstances and environment. From that information you can make the best choices for your pets.

Make sure your goats have ample time each day to be moving around and eating what they find. You can add hay to the open spaces too for them to have plenty to eat. Even if you don't have fields for them, you should scatter their food sources around an open area. It is in their nature to move around and eat.

Portions for Each Goat

Feeding should take place twice per day. Divide the total amount of food for the goats and give them one part of it at each feeding. Keep a good eye on your goats and feeding times. You need to be observant of those who tend to consume more than their own share of the food.

Don't assume each of the goats gets enough to eat. You need to be positive that is happening. It is possible for them to all eat well but some won't develop the same size of weight and height due to genetic factors. However, you don't want to assume those differences are due to those factors. You need to rule out the possibility that certain goats eat more than their fair share.

If that happens, you may need to section off the goats for feeding times. This ensures each goat only has access to their own food. It helps with ensuring none of them overeat while others aren't getting the amount of nutrients they need to thrive.

Hay

The overall feeding amounts will depend on the age of your goats. Males need more food than females. The exception is when the females are pregnant or nursing their young. These goats can thrive on a diet that is mainly hay. Make sure the hay is sweet smelling, and free of dust. Legume hay is the best choice as it is easiest for them to digest.

Adult Nigerian Dwarf goats will consume 1 or 2 pounds of hay per day. With that in mind, make sure you have plenty readily available. However, all food sources including hay should be out of their reach other than the amount you allocate to feed them. Otherwise, they are quite opportunistic and will eat far too much.

Hay should be alfalfa, Bermuda, or a blend of the two for your goats. This is the best type of food resource for their stomach to digest. These forms of hay have longer stems and that aids in the overall digestion process. These forms of hay are also more natural than alternatives.

Hay is going to cost you a bit more but it is worth it for the overall health and well-being of your Nigerian Dwarf goats. It is also messy but the clean up isn't difficult or time consuming if you do it regularly. Try to buy organic too to avoid any types of pesticide residue being on the hay you feed them.

Pellets

You can also offer your goats pellets made from alfalfa, Bermuda, or a blend. It is a bit cheaper than hay and it is much easier to clean up. You don't have to worry about any waste either. You will need to wash it with water if you don't buy an organic variety. This washing process can help to remove any residue from pesticides that may be lingering.

Even though you save some money, your goats don't get the same nutritional value from it. As a result, pellets can reduce their overall health. This is why I strongly suggest you go with the hay rather than the pellets for feeding them.

Grains

You can give younger male goats grains but once they are about 6 months old cut it back to very little. If you allow them to have much after they are a year old they are going to be prone to kidney infections which are quite painful. Females do need grain so you may need to separate them for feeding purposes. You can give the males some fruit now and then to help compensate for not giving them the grain.

I do know some owners of Nigerian Dwarf goats who give males grain. However, they add urine acidifier called Ammonium

Chloride to the grain. This will help to reduce the health risks. If you don't have enough space to separate the males and females or pasture for them to graze often this can be a good solution to consider.

Grain is considered to be a dietary supplement for goats. Therefore, it can be given WITH hay but it should be given IN PLACE OF the hay. This is important information to remember. I give my Nigerian Dwarf goats grains because it helps keep milk production levels at this highest possible.

My vet also told me pregnant goats need the grain to assist them with creating milk production for their offspring. Since they can have up to 4 offspring at a time, it is quite important for them to produce enough milk.

Early on with our goats, we had to bottle feed some of the kids. Once I added grain to the diet though I haven't had to do so. First-hand knowledge that it does make a difference! Ideally, you want to buy a good quality goat feed grain with at least 12% to protein. I buy products with 18% protein. Avoid any products that contain urea as it can make your goats sick.

Low Protein/Low Calcium Diet

Since males are prone to UTIs and kidney problems if they have too much protein or too much calcium, control it. I just feed my males and females the same thing. They get a low protein, low calcium diet daily.

This is a very important point to keep in mind. I have read numerous times on forums about males with kidney problems. Their owners don't realize they are prone to them. This is information you need to make good feeding decisions for your goats. It is also puzzling to me that people aren't' getting this information from their vet.

Introduce Dietary Changes Slowly

Your Nigerian Dwarf goats are going to become stressed, engage in difficult behaviors, and may not produce milk if you change their diet suddenly. Any types of changes need to be done slowly. Introduce anything new in a small amount so they can get used to it.

You can't expect a goat to be able to change its diet and not suffer. The worst thing you can do is change it from being a browser in the pasture to feeding it grain all the time in an enclosure. Your vet will be coming out to help soon because your goats are going to get sick. Their digestive systems won't be able to handle such changes.

Water

Your goats should have access to fresh water all the time. They will drink often and it needs to be there for them. In the winter months, I go out in the mornings and chip away the ice so they can get to the water. In the summer, I add big blocks of ice to the water tank to keep it cool.

Make sure you clean the water containers regularly too. Otherwise, they can develop germs and bacteria that make your goats ill. If your goats run out of water they will become stressed. They may fight and they may not eat because of it. Water allows the stomach to ferment and to properly digest food.

Keep in mind when your females are lactating, they will increase their water intake daily. All of your goats will drink more water when the temperatures warm up. Keep a good eye on water availability so they never go without or fight over access to what is offered.

Extras

While you will find your goats enjoy a variety of extra foods, offer them in moderation. They should be a grand treat on occasion rather than something they get on a regular basis. Some of the extras we offer to our goats include:
- Salt blocks
- Fruits
- Vegetables
- Baked Goods
- Tree prunings from pine, spruce, and apple trees

Concentrates and Supplements

Don't get yourself worked up about concentrates and supplements. Now, you don't have to offer any of them to your goats but I recommend you do use them. Of course if you are going to take such a route you need to know what they need. There is no exact information I can offer you about that because each goat is different. Each season can also influence changes.

For adult males, I offer ½ pound of concentrate. For adult females I offer 1 pound of concentrate for every 2 quarts of milk produced. When it comes to salt, make sure it doesn't contain copper because your goats will be very sensitive to it. You can leave the salt blocks out all the time. Your goats will know how much their bodies need at any given point in time.

Enteroxotemia

Overeating can be very dangerous for your goats. Not only does it make it harder for them to move around, it increases the risk of serious health issues. The heart will have to work harder and that can reduce quality of life as well as years of life.

Enteroxotemia is a serious medical disease for Nigerian Dwarf goats which is the result of overeating. Goats may binge on various food sources so you have to make sure they have hay available. You also have to make sure they get their vaccinations timely. Both will reduce this risk.

Carefully rationing the amount of food the goats have access to each day is important. It is one of the biggest responsibilities of caring for such animals as pets. If you don't have the time for them you shouldn't get them. If you have to be away from home for even a day, someone you trust must be able to care for them.

Genetics

Studies show the quality of the food your Nigerian Dwarf goats consume is very important for their offspring. When they are offered the right balance of nutrients they are more fertile and overall healthier. They are more likely to give birth to offspring who are strong and healthy too. Even if your goal isn't to breed these goats, you want to offer them a chance at the very best quality of life possible.

The birth weight of offspring can be up to 50% higher when the mother is eating a quality diet. As a result, your young goats are less likely to have health issues or to die soon after birth. A high protein diet can also help your goats to have more energy and to live a long and happy life.

Chapter 9 - Daily Care

Hopefully by this time in the book, you are thinking how much fun Nigerian Dwarf goats are. Plus, you are thinking about the daily care they require. I know I have said it more than once thus far… but if you don't have the time or the compassion to give to them they aren't going to make a good pet for you. They require daily care.

You can't get them and then start to neglect the responsibility once the novelty has worn off. You may find you have to get out of bed an hour earlier to take care of them in the mornings. You may not like the concept of shoveling up their bodily excretions. Yet this is all part of the daily care you are committing to as an owner of Nigerian Dwarf goats.

Most people are motivated to do the work, and I hope you will be too. If you already have too much on your plate though it may not work out. You have to identify where you can cut back to fit the needs of the goats in. We all get the same 24 hours to work with each day.

Think about your own physical abilities too. If you have a hard time getting around it may be impossible for you to successfully commit to the daily care of the goats. I have a friend who had to get rid of his due to the progression of his arthritis concerns. There were days it was hard enough for him to get out of bed and showered. He just couldn't take care of his goats any longer.

Assessing

Take a few minutes to assess and observe your goats each morning. I do this each time I feed them. Are they acting friendly and happy? Is there anything out of the ordinary? As you get to know the personality of each of your Nigerian Dwarf goats, you will quickly identify something that is off. If you have quite a few goats, do a head count each morning too.

The more you pay attention to your goats, the easier it is to notice something just isn't right with them. Think about your kids for a moment. You know their usual temperament and patterns of behavior. When they start to act out of sync with that you know something is up.

You may ask them how they feel and reach for the thermometer. You can't ask your goats how they feel but you can check their stools, check their temperature, and monitor their movements. You can also pay attention to how much food and water they are drinking.

In recent years, my wife and I come up with the idea of installing some cameras in the areas of our goats. When we notice one isn't doing too well, we can go back and check footage from the night before. It allows us to pinpoint when the symptoms may have started.

This is an additional expense, and not required but I do recommend it. This can also help if you have identified fencing problems. The footage can show you the goat or goats responsible for the issue. If you have suspicions there are territorial issues in place among your herd you can monitor their behaviors.

I suggest this because they may change how they act when you or other humans are around. They may not display the signs of aggression until it comes to where they stay in the shelter or the food and water that is being consumed.

I also like the peace of mind these cameras offer for protecting my goats. If another person comes on my property to bother them or we have potential predators lurking around I can address those problems quickly and efficiently.

Feeding and Watering

Set out the food for your goats twice per day. By dividing it, you reduce health risks associated with overeating by goats. Check the water levels and make sure there is more than enough fresh water to last all of the goats until the next feeding time.

I won't go into more detail here about feeding and watering because that has all been disclosed well in a previous chapter. However, you need to plan well for things that come up. For example, what are you going to do when you go on vacation or away for the holidays?

You can't just leave tons of extra food and water around for your goats. That can lead to serious problems! We belong to a network of Nigerian Dwarf goat owners in our area. We help each other out when other families are gone and it works well. This ensures feeding and watering get done like they should. It also ensures a human is checking on the goats twice per day.

I encourage you to make such connections with other owners in your area. You can also hire someone such as your neighbor or a friend you trust to take care of your goats in your absence. Make sure they come do the rounds with you enough that they know what to do on their own when you are gone.

Without such contacts, you may feel like you can never get any time away. You don't want that to be the case. You need to enjoy your vacation time and your holidays. You don't want to be resentful of your beautiful goats. There are always solutions but you just need to plan well and plan early to make it all work.

Grooming

Take a few minutes each day to groom your goats. Keep brushes handy and take a few minutes to complete this task. I will tell you from personal experience it is so much easier to do this daily than to work with matted goats because you neglected this part of their care for days or weeks at a time.

Use quality brushes designed to work well with the coat of goats. Brush to get deep into the coat but not hard enough to hurt the goat. Brushing well removes loose hair and to remove any signs of dandruff. It also increases blood flow which in turn will make the skin and the coat healthier.

While brushing, use your hands to check for any signs of abnormalities. They can be hidden by the coat. If you identify any lumps, bumps, or swelling you need to contact your vet for further investigation.

Brush in the direction of the coat. Start at the neck and then work your way down their back. Next, move along both sides. Make sure you don't skip the legs or the abdominal area.

Many people ask about bathing Nigerian Dwarf goats and the answer is you don't have to do it! However, I recommend a bath every 4 months or so. This will help to remove any dirt and debris that has accumulated. If your goats get lice you will definitely need to bathe them after the medicine has been applied to their coat.

Use warm water if you bathe your goats, they don't like cold water. Use shampoo that is designed specifically for goats. Since they aren't going to want to go into the water, use a collar and lease to secure them in place. I secure them to a milk stand and then bathe them.

Interaction

Even though your goats get to interact with each other, they need to do so with humans as well. If you want them to be awesome pets, you need to play with them and nurture them. You can also train them with some simple commands. We will cover that more in a future chapter.

66

If you don't spend time with your goats, their social development can be hindered. Some owners worry that too much interaction with them changes their natural instincts. That isn't true, but they have been domesticated since they were bred and human interactions are a part of their natural instincts.

Milking

If you plan to have Nigerian Dwarf goats for milk or milk based products, you need to plan to spend some time each day for this task. Milking is easier for these miniature goats than with full size goats or cows. However, it still takes time and you need to develop a system. I will cover this too in more detail in a later chapter.

Chapter 10 - Seasonal Care

It is important to create a calendar of seasonal care needs for your goats. When you buy goats at different times or have offspring, then the needs can be based on specific goats. I have a calendar that is for the goats only. This prevents it from getting too tangled up due to our busy household schedule too.

I write down each goats name and what they may need such as vaccines or other types of care. Then I don't forget what needs to be taken care of. With some needs such as deworming though they all get the medicine for it the same day so having it on the calendar is very simple.

Once your goats are all about a year old, you can get them on the same schedule for worming and vaccines. Any time you bring new goats to your herd, make sure they are dewormed and they are current on vaccines. Doing so will save you plenty of issues and concerns.

When I have females who are pregnant, I also write down on my calendar when I think she is due. This is a general timeframe but I always try to make sure I am around during those final weeks should she need any assistance. I certainly don't want to be on vacation when she gives birth. Usually the birthing process is trouble free but I like to be there for my goats just in case.

I also write down the dates that the offspring were born. This helps me to schedule their first vaccines and to schedule a time to remove the horns. I know when they are about 8 weeks of age the mother will be weaning them.

That means I need to think about food for the young ones in addition to my other goats I have to care for. It means an increase in my budget for such items. If I am going to sell the offspring, I can put it on my calendar the date to start advertising them.

Scheduling is very simple when you have a calendar in place that is specific to your goats. I have 4 goats right now so I use a different color of marker for each of them. I also use another color to write down anything that pertains to my entire herd.

Hooves

When it comes to seasonal care, the hooves are one of the most important. This is also one of the least expensive parts of their care. It doesn't take too much time to do it once you get the hang of it. If you don't take good care of the hooves you will have huge health care expenses to contend with for your goats.

The hooves for your goats should be trimmed every 3 months or so. This will help them to walk evenly and to prevent them from tripping and falling. Failure to trim them can result in a permanent limp.

Get a good trimming tool that is designed specifically for the hooves of goats. Apply very little pressure and take a tiny bit off the hooves at a time. You can do more as you need to but going slowly prevents you from taking off too much.

Growing up on a farm, I learned how to take care of the hooves of Nigerian Dwarf goats at a young age. However, I realize not everyone has had such an opportunity. I suggest watching videos online to get you get a good idea of what the process entails.

Disbudding

When you buy baby goats or your goats have offspring, you need to take part in disbudding. This is the process of removing their horns. It should be done by the time they are 2 weeks of age. Feel the area and you should remove them when you can feel the buds. If you wait until you can see them, the horns have already attached to the head. This makes it very hard to stop it from growing.

69

You will need to shave the area so you can see the width of the base of the horn nubs. I have also found shaving a wide path means you don't have to smell burning hair!

Place the disbudding tool over each bud for about 15 seconds. Use even pressure and slowly move in a circular motion with it. You can remove the tool when you see a copper ring and the white of the skull underneath.

This doesn't hurt the young goat, but it does scare them. The burnt smell can also make them skittish. I spend a few minutes comforting them and loving them. Then I take them back to their mother. I have learned to do so bottom first rather than face first. This prevents the mother goat from smelling the burnt hair. She may push her baby away for a few hours until the smell goes away.

Clipping

Once a year you should clip your goats. The shorter hair is going to help them stay cool. It also allows the sunlight to be able to get to their skin. The sunlight can prevent lice and various critters from infiltrating their skin and coat. Of course you don't want to clip them in the fall or winter because they can get too cold. Do so in the spring or the early part of summer.

The tail should be clipped for the females before they give birth. This will reduce the amount of blood and fluid that can stick to the tail. Remove hair from the udders if you find that you have hairs getting into the milk often.

Vaccinations

It is your responsibility when you buy goats to find out if they have their first set of vaccinations or not. If they do, you should get decimation at the time of your purchase. If they don't, you need to get it done. They should get a CD/T when they are 8 weeks old. All goats should be vaccinated annually as part of the preventative care schedule.

Depending on where you live, your vet may suggest other vaccines on an annual basis. They know what they are talking about so you should listen. Some of those vaccines are optional but if they tell you they are a good idea then I would make them a mandatory part of the annual care for your Nigerian Dwarf goats.

Chapter 11 - Tips for Buying Nigerian Dwarf Goats

If your decision is to buy Nigerian Dwarf goats, make time to get a great deal. You want a fair price but you always want quality goats. Make sure you know about regulations, zoning, and licensing requirements for your area. They aren't all the same and you don't want to get into legal trouble.

While a great deal of this information is covered in an early chapter, keep in mind it changes often. With that in mind, you can take what I provide you and use it as a foundation to start exploring and gathering information. Make sure you always check the regulations and zoning where you live. Get the proper licensing.

Just because you read it here NOW doesn't mean that is how it will play out 6 months or a year from now. It is your responsibility to make sure you are following the current laws. It is also your responsibility to make sure you are well informed about the goats before you purchase any. Don't be in a rush because that often leads to regrets.

Nothing is more upsetting than discovering you got taken for a ride when you purchased your goats. I have seen it happen to so many people, and it makes me quite upset. The decision to own goats is hard enough and then someone makes it even tougher on you because they were more interested in money than anything else.

Ideally, you want to find a seller that stands behind the offer they give. If they sell the goats as is that always makes me suspicious. It makes me think they know something I don't and they want to make sure I don't come back to ask for my money.

Investigate Breeders

Not all breeders of Nigerian Dwarf goats are following the laws and the regulations. Not all of them offer the best conditions for the goats to be cared for. You need to make sure they are following all regulations and have applicable licensing.

Some of these breeders are a money making machine, but they don't care at all about the goats. They don't spend time interacting with them and they buy them the cheapest food sources they can. They cut corners on vaccines and they breed the females again and again which isn't good for their health. It is just too much on their bodies.

Take the time to ask the seller questions and to go to the site to see how the goats are cared for. Ask to see the parents of offspring. If they aren't willing to show you around, that should be taken as a red flag they have something to hide. If they try to rush you into making a purchase, that should also make you think about what they don't want you to find out.

If they offer you a discounted price if you buy the goats right then, don't fall for it. You may be thinking you just got a steal. However, if they really feel their goats are worth the asking price then they will hold out to get that amount. Don't let them tell you other people are looking too as a ploy to get you to buy in a hurry either.

The truth is if those Nigerian Dwarf goats are gone when you are ready to buy them you will just need to keep looking. If you are happy with that particular breeder you can wait until they have more offspring ready to go. Otherwise, search for other reputable sellers.

Read reviews from other buyers to see what they think of particular breeders. Such information will really help you to find a great deal. Now, I am not a breeder but I do sell goats from time to time. These are the offspring of our goats, and I simply can't keep all of them.

However, I let people come to my place to see how my goats are cared for. I let them see the offspring and I am very open about the transaction that will take place. I have even turned potential buyers away! I ask plenty of questions too and if they don't seem to have the patience or the knowledge yet for the goats I don't want them to have them. They can go buy from someone else I guess, but at least I sleep well at night knowing my goats are sold to people I feel will take very good care of them.

They should be able to provide you with the paperwork relating to your goats when you buy them. Don't let them tell you they will mail you the papers later on. Sadly, I have seen that happen to friends and the papers never arrive. There is no recourse for them after the sale is made. As a result, it makes it harder for you to resell any of the offspring from your goats if you don't have those papers.

If the papers aren't ready, kindly ask them to hold the goats for you and you will come back for them when the papers are ready. They may ask you to provide a deposit to hold them. Don't pay in cash, give them a check. This is your proof of the deposit funds being given to them. You also want a written contract signed by them before you hand over that check.

On a side note, if you notice something that just isn't right with any Nigerian Dwarf goat breeder, don't ignore it. You have a responsibility to report it. Not only for the well-being of the goats but also to prevent other potential buyers from becoming victims of their unethical and illegal practices.

Don't ignore awful practices because you can get goats from them for a low price. It isn't fair to these animals and you will be just as guilty as those breeders are because you choose to look the other way.

Comparing Prices

There is a continued demand for Nigerian Dwarf goats and it seems to grow and grow. That demand mixed with the value of some variations means the prices can be all over the place. We have sold some of our kids because we don't want to have too many goats. Once they can be weaned from their mothers we sell them for a decent price.

This money goes back into the ongoing care of the goats we do keep. It can help to pay for their food, supplies, shelter, and medical care. However, those that breed these goats for a business are continually after the process of providing the best possible genetics. With that in mind, you will pay premium prices for top notch goats.

Always take the time to compare prices so you know what they are worth. I have seen them go for three times what they were worth. However, someone bought them because they didn't do their homework. On the other side of the coin, if you see a price that is substantially lower than the rest you should be asking them why they aren't charging more.

Goats with blue eyes are always worth more than those with other colors. Keep this in mind when you are shopping around. If you plan to resell Nigerian Dwarf goats you want to invest in stock with blue eyes. It will make your offspring more desirable and more profitable.

Evaluating the Stock

Ask about the genetics of the goats you think about purchasing. When I sell them, I always show the potential customers who the parents are. They can see the physical traits and the quality of health of these animals in my care.

Seeing a pair of healthy and beautiful parents is enticing to those wishing to buy goats. It helps them to see the potential for the offspring they are thinking about owning. Of course there can be variations from the parents to the offspring due to the genetic markers but at least it is something to encourage them with.

Vaccinations

Never buy goats who haven't been properly vaccinated. If you do, there is a good chance they will be unhealthy. This can result in huge expenses for you that weren't budgeted for. It can also result in your goats dying soon after you purchase them.

If vaccinations have been given, ask for verification. This should include the type of vaccine, the date of the vaccine, and who administered it. If you have goats at home and bring home another that doesn't have vaccines it could very risky for your established herd.

How Many to Purchase

Always have at least two Nigerian Dwarf goats. One is going to be very sad and lonely. You can shower it with attention daily but it won't be enough to make up for the social interaction with their peers which is instinctive. If you don't want to have babies to deal with, get all of the same gender.

The number to purchase depends on how much time and money you wish to put into them as pets. It also depends on if you have plans to breed and resell these miniature goats. The amount of space you have for them is also something to think about. I wouldn't suggest getting too many at once or you may feel overwhelmed.

You can start out with a low number and gradually add more to your herd over time. You can choose to purchase them or you can allow pairs of your Nigerian Dwarf goats to breed and then keep some or all of the offspring.

Males or Females

Think about the pros and cons before you decide on the gender of your goats. Females are often more expensive because they offer milk and the ability to produce more goats. If you plan to enjoy milk from the goats you want a couple of females. I don't recommend depending on just one female for all of the production.

Of course if you plan to have offspring you will need at least one male and one female. If you don't wish to have any offspring you can get all females, and enjoy the milk production. It isn't recommended to have all males though as they can become quite aggressive and territorial with each other.

Ongoing Cost of Providing for them

Spend some time allocating a budget for the startup and the ongoing costs of caring for your goats. What will you need to create a large enough enclosure for them that offers them all their needs met day after day? How much will it cost you per month for food and for vaccines?

Don't forget to budget for extras such as emergency fencing repairs or when you have to call the vet to care for a sick goat. You don't want to be stressed about these costs that come out of left field.

Baby Goats

You can buy a baby goat as young as 8 weeks old. It has been weaned from the mother and they are the least expensive most of the time. Part of the reason is most of the breeders typically have tons of baby goats all at the same time. They tend to offer deals if you buy several of them so keep that in mind.

The down side to this is it will be about 1 ½ years before you can breed them. Add in another 6 months for you to start getting milk and it will be about 2 years for that production. If you already have some mature females it may not matter much to you. If you are just getting started with your goat population though it can make a difference.

The cost should range between $150 and $300 USD/ £100 and £200 for a baby Nigerian Dwarf goat. Keep in mind this is just a general guideline area though. The actual cost will depend on many factors including:

- Parental genetics
- Breeder
- Milking star awards
- Coloring of coat
- Eye coloring (blue eyes will usually cost the most)

When shopping for baby goats, pay attention to their personality. It is a good idea to buy those displaying friendly characteristics. You want to avoid those who seem to be afraid of everything or to be too head strong because they may not interact well with other goats.

Junior Goats

You may be able to find junior goats. This category includes those who aren't babies anymore but they aren't fully mature either. They are usually between 6 months and 1 year of age. This includes females who are mature but they haven't mated yet.

If you want them to be bred before you purchase them, they will cost more. However, you will have offspring to add to your herd in about 5 months. You will also have access to fresh goat milk from them in about 5 months too. You can usually find junior goats for sale from breeds between $400 and $600 USD/£260 and £390. Again, there are several factors that influence price.

Find females who aren't afraid to eat out of your hand. When possible, ask to see the mother of the females you are interested in. Check out the size of their teats as this will influence milk production. Don't rely just on the teat size of females you look to buy. They will always be smaller before she has given birth at least once.

Senior Doe

Perhaps you are interested in buying an older female goat who can offer you milk as soon as you take her home. Many of them are great producers and you won't have any problems with them. However, there are some out there very stubborn and they are set in their ways. They are going to be hard for you to control because they aren't going to adjust well to a new living environment.

They vary in price from $200 to $500 USD/ £130 to £325 depending on milk production and their behaviors. Make sure you ask lots of questions so you don't end up with one that nobody wanted due to problems. If the price is very low, it is important to question why. Make sure she isn't fearful of everything. Check out her teats as they should be at least 1 ½ inches in length. Check for signs of skin disorders and infections.

Males

You may be interested in males for breeding, and they can be expensive. They can be sold from $400 to $1,000 USD / £260 to £650. It depends on their genetics and identifying markers. Males are valuable because they produce the sperm needed to create offspring. If you shop around for a male make sure you take your time to identify one that can help you generate your own herd over time.

Transporting

It amazes me how many people go to buy goats but don't think about how they will get them home. Some breeders or sellers are able to take them for you but they usually charge fees. I have sold young offspring and transported for people that live within a 30 mile radius. Further than that though just takes too much of time my time and gas to justify the sell.

If you know you are going to buy goats, be prepared to transport them. Take along some carriers with you. If you decide to leave the location with the goats you will have what you need. If you leave without buying, you will need those items for when you do buy the goats.

If you are buying baby goats, a small pet carrier for each of them is more than sufficient. You can also use dog crates if you have them available. Make sure the size of the carrier is going to be sufficient for the age and size of the goat. You don't want them to be too crowded in there. If they have too much open space, they may become anxious on the ride home.

If you plan to put the carrier or crate in the back of a pickup, make sure you put down straw or would shavings to offer some bedding. Cover the tops with a tarp or blankets if it is cold out to prevent the wind from getting to your goats.

You can place the carriers or crates in the back of a vehicle such as your SUV or minivan. If you have a backseat that folds down, that is an option too. For baby goats you can even place the smaller carriers in the back seating area. Cover the bottom of these carriers or crates with a blanket to help them be comfortable.

I do know some people who hold them on their lap on the way home. I don't recommend this as it can be dangerous to the safety of the goat. It can also be dangerous to the driver of the vehicle. You don't know if the goat will get spooked and bolt around the car. In an instant this can occur and you won't have any warning.

If you do hold a goat on your lap, make sure you have a towel between you and then. They may poop or pee on the route home. Hold them securely in place with two hands to reduce the chances of them getting away from you and loose in the vehicle while it is moving.

You should stop at least every 3 hours on your ride back with the goats. Get them out of the car so they can walk around a bit. This helps to balance their equilibrium again. Allow them to get some food, some water, and to eliminate bodily waste.

Getting your Goats Settled

Your goats are going to be both scared and nervous when you first take them home. Give them plenty of extra comfort measures. Talk to them softly and allow them to run around and explore their new environment. They may be extra noisy or extremely quiet the first few days until they settle in so be patient with them.

They may not eat or drink as much as you feel they should for the first couple of weeks. Talk to your goats as you approach their shelter. They will start to get used to you and not run off when you come out there. Don't chase them around their enclosure as they will see this as a game.

Encourage them to come to you and they will do so in time. Make sure they have access to food, water, and daily exercise. A routine for them is important so they feel safe and they feel comfortable in their new living environment.

It is strongly encouraged that you quarantine your new Nigerian Dwarf goats from the rest of your herd for 30 days. If you don't already have goats at home then this won't pertain to you. Separating the two groups though is a precaution so you can prevent any concerns from the new goats from becoming an issue for the goats you already have.

If you don't notice any problems after 30 days it is safe to say they are healthy and they can be implemented with the other goats. Make sure your structure for the goats is designed to provide you with the separation option without difficulty so you don't feel like you have no choice but to all them all to integrate when you bring the new goats home.

Signs of Stress

Even if you offer the ideal living conditions for your new goats, they can be suffering due to stress. Identifying the signs of stress is very important. The process of transporting them may be when you notice the problem. They may become very vocal. This could be their first time away from the herd they have known such birth so be patient with them.

Even with older goats, you have to keep an eye on stress. They may be in a new location where you feed them different food than what they used to get. It can take time for their bodies to get used to those dietary changes. They may be stressed because they have lost their position in the hierarchy of their old herd. They will have to establish a position in this new location.

Keep a good eye on the interactions between the goats. Most of the time it goes smoothly with very little aggression. However, that isn't always the way it works out. There can be goats who are aggressive bullies and you need to make sure they don't harass other goats. If they do, you need to work on training them or you need to get rid of them.

Depression can occur due to the stress and they may not eat or drink much. Take some time to sit with these goats and feed them out of your hand if you need to. They should snap out of this state in a few days but if they don't talk to your vet.

If your goat is experiencing diarrhea or pneumonia soon after you bring them home, it may not be due to their physical well-being. These health problems can be brought on because the high level of stress can reduce the effectiveness of the immune system. Contact your vet right away so they can help with the recovery process.

Chapter 12 - Breeding Options

Since breeding is a common concept for those who own Nigerian Dwarf goats, I wanted to include a chapter about it. However, I want to make sure you understand this will just be a brief overview. This is a book about these goats as pets and not about breeding.

If you would like to find out more about this particular topic, I do encourage you to get a book that is specifically going to cover the ins and outs of it before you get started. Doing so will help you to decide if it is an investment of time and money you are up for.

Year Round Option

These goats are able to take part in breeding all year long. As long as their basic needs are met they will do so. However, most breeders limit the number of times it occurs. Ideally, a doe should only give birth twice every 3 years. A break of at least 6 months is recommended between pregnancies to allow her body time to recover.

There are breeders out there though getting the females pregnant over and over again as quickly as they can. You don't want to buy your Nigerian Dwarf goats from such breeders. You certainly don't want to become one either that engages in such practices to make a few extra bucks. Your priority should always be about the overall care and well-being of these animals.

Selective Breeding Pairs

Genetics are key to being a successful breeder of these goats. With that in mind, you may have to create the ideal conditions for a selective pair of them to breed. This can include secluding them away from other goats. Males will compete for the right to mate with females. Keeping males separated and only allowing the access to the females you want them to mate with may be part of the process you need to engage in.

Few Problems

Even though Nigerian Dwarf goats are small in size, they don't have too many birthing problems. Most of the time the females are able to get pregnant, carry their offspring, and have the young without incident.

Offspring

The offspring can be in liters up to 4 per pregnancy. They can weigh from 1 to 2 pounds at birth. The young grow very quickly due to the high fat content in their mother's milk. Typically, these goats are very good mothers and take wonderful care of the young. They will be weaned at around 8 weeks of age.

In instances where they can't properly care for the young you may need to bottle feed them. This can occur if the mother loses interest in her young, she isn't producing enough milk, or she has health concerns that prevent her from taking on the responsibility of her young.

Selling Responsibly

If you are a breeder of Nigerian Dwarf goats, you have very big shoes to fill. There is a demand for them but you always want to uphold the integrity of these animals. With that in mind, you need to make sure their basic needs are met at all times. You also need to fully disclose any information you have to potential buyers.

Keep in mind if you are found to violate the laws, you can end up in legal trouble. You can have your breeding rights removed. You may be fined or face jail time. You may have to appear in court for legal proceedings or for civil suit proceedings.

Caring for a Pregnant Doe

Regardless of breeding or pets, Nigerian Dwarf goats who are pregnant need to be taken care of properly. It takes about 5 months for the young to be born. You can milk the doe until the last 2 months before she gives birth. The female will start to dry up in terms of milk production.

While this will occur naturally, you should do your part to encourage it to happen. Instead of milking daily you should start to milk every other day for a couple of weeks. Then go to every 3 days. When you have that timeframe, don't drink the milk. It will have too much of a salty taste due to the buildup of minerals.

You will need to make sure you deworm them about 2 months before they give birth. If you don't, there is a high risk they can get worms. This will hinder the development of their offspring. It can result in mortality at birth and very low birth weight. It can also result in offspring born with worms you will have to take care of.

Supplement the diet of a female who is pregnant in the last 6 weeks of pregnancy. Offer her some extras such as fruit and vegetables to boost her level of nutrition. Avoid giving pregnant females too much grain as it can be harder for them to digest in the later stages of pregnancy. I don't give my pregnant females any grain for the last month of pregnancy as a precautionary measure.

A few weeks before the female gives birth, check her by running your fingers along her spine to her tail. Squeeze the ligament before you reach her tail. Check it daily and you will notice it starts to become more relaxed as the days go by. When she is about to give birth it will be completely relaxed.

Delivery generally goes very easily for Nigerian Dwarf goats but that isn't always the case. I try to be there when they go into labor and give birth in case there are any complications and I can call my vet. We had our goats for 4 years before we had a scenario where something just didn't seem right and we called our vet to assist.

After Birth

Once the offspring is born, give the mother time alone with them. She will need time to bond and to lick them clean. When you know birth is close, it is best to seclude her from other goats in your herd. If the young baby isn't latching on to drink milk within an hour of birth then you may need to assist it. If the problem can't be resolved you may need to bottle feed that little one.

A new mother may reject feeding one, several, or all of her offspring. It could be due to her not producing enough milk. Sometimes, it is a single baby goat who has trouble suckling on teats. If you need to bottle feed, give them up to 1 ounce of milk 3 times per day for the first couple of weeks.

I tried several different types of nipples for bottles. It wasn't until we located Pritchard nipples (the red ones) that they seemed to really work well. I have had a few baby goats who couldn't suckle enough for the nipples. For those, you will need to use feeding tubes.

My vet is wonderful about assisting with this and you will need a qualified professional for those young ones if they are going to survive. Warm milk is the best for bottle feeding the young. If it is too cold they aren't going to drink it. Rub the top of the baby goat's head while you are giving them the bottle. This trick will get them to open their mouth so they suckle rather than pushing the nipple back out.

Pasteurized goat milk is best to feed these young to help kill any possible bacteria. Heat the milk in a double boiler to 165 degrees F. Allow the milk to reduce in temperature so it is warm but not too hot for the goat to consume it.

Watch mom for several days after birth. She should be eating, drinking water, producing milk for her offspring, and taking good care of them. If she isn't producing enough milk talk to your vet. You may need to bottle feed them to make sure they get enough nutrition to thrive.

Ethical Practices

There are complete books and courses out there to help you with breeding if you wish to go that direction. Make sure you are always engaged in ethical practices should you be a breeder. Never mislead people about what they are getting from you. Never compromise the health and the happiness of any goats to make a profit.

Chapter 13 - How to Extract Milk

If you have never milked a goat before you may be a bit intimidated by the process. I promise you it won't be hard and you will reap fantastic benefits from doing so. The milk offered from Nigerian Dwarf goats is amazing!

My family drinks it daily and we often make a variety of products from it. While we got our goats as pets, growing up we drank this milk too. I have to say this was one of the reasons why I wanted to have them around. My wife was a bit skeptical but it wasn't long before she was out there milking them with me.

In this chapter, we are going to cover the basics of milking your goats. You want to do it gently and correctly. Females can start producing milk after they are mature and they become pregnant. The young in her body is what will create the milk production process.

The amount of milk she will produce is going to decrease over time. When she has young to feed, it will be the highest. They are weaned around 2 months of age but she will still produce milk daily. After about a year though the milk production will stop. She will need to breed again in order to stimulate the milk production.

You can milk a pregnant doe. However, you should avoid doing so in the last 2 months of the pregnancy. This allows her to build up nutrients and immune system builders for her offspring.

Milk Production Guidelines

You may be curious about the overall production of milk from each mature female goat. You can get about 2 quarts per day, but it varies based on the creature and their environment. Some produce more and others produce far less. As you get to know your goats and you tweak their diet you will be able to get the maximum amount of milk they are able to offer.

When the females are ready to give birth they have more milk production than at other times. This is to help them with offering enough to feed their offspring. It is recommended to separate the young from their mother at night. This allows her to fill up with milk.

You can then milk her in the morning and then let the milk she has the rest of the day be offered to the young. However, if you don't think she has enough to offer them you should stop taking milk for your use and allow it all to go to their consumption.

However, they have a body designed to hold back milk for their young. When the young are about 8 weeks old, she will wean them. You can then go back to milking the female in the morning and at night. This is when you will be able to accumulate up to ½ a gallon of milk per day from her.

You will notice over time though the milk production decreases. It is usually a small amount of decrease over weeks and the next several months. About 6 months after giving birth you may notice the production is about 6 cups per day. About 9 months after giving birth it may be down to a quart per day.

Milking Process

Don't be nervous about milking your Nigerian Dwarf goats. Plan plenty of time for it at first until you get the hang of it. As I mentioned, you should milk them in the morning and again in the evening. Try to do it at the same time each day if possible.

Make sure the pails you use for the milk are clean. They should be rinsed well and free of any residue. Milking the goats doesn't hurt them at all. I know I was scared of causing them pain. What you need to know is if you don't milk them they will experience pain and discomfort. The milking process actually offers them relief.

Don't tug on the teat in order to milk your goats. Instead, you want to trap the milk inside of the teat. Use your thumb and the finger right next to it and create a pinching element at the bottom of the teat. At the same time, use your other fingers to generate pressure on the teat.

Now, at first the muscles in your fingers aren't going to be strong for this type of activity. It sounds silly but you will know exactly what I mean when you start milking your goats. This is why it will take you about ½ an hour to milk each one at first. As those muscles in your fingers develop and get strong, you will be able to it in about 5 to 10 minutes.

Items you Need

There are a few items you will need to aid you with milking your Nigerian Dwarf goats. Here is what I use:

- Milking stand
- Stool
- Buckets
- Udder cleaner
- Strip cups
- Filtering system
- Storage containers

I don't recommend getting on your hands and knees to milk your goats. It isn't going to allow you good visibility of the teats. It can also be hard on your body. I have found it doesn't give me the control I need to successful milk.

Invest in a few good milking stands and you will be all set. I got those with a ramp so the goat can walk up and then I secure them in place with a collar and leash. I place a stool behind the goat and get to work. This gives me plenty of visibility and control. It also means I am not putting stress on my back or my knees which I appreciate at my age!

Always use stainless steel buckets. If you use plastic buckets your milk won't taste right. It will also be harder for you to keep them clean and sanitary. There aren't any pores in stainless steel. As a result, dirt and bacteria can hide when you try to clean and sterilize them. They will also last a very long time.

I have several stainless steel buckets I use only for the purpose of milking my goats. They cost about $10 USD/ £7 each and they last forever. Try to find those with a lid when possible. Until I found those, I covered the top of the bucket with a clean towel. Then I fastened it to the ridge with clothes pins as I carried it from the goat pens to the house.

I run our stainless steel buckets through the dishwasher in the house a couple of times per week. I certainly don't want to take any risk that the milk will have health risks for my family by consuming it. The heat in the dishwasher gets significantly hotter than water from my faucet to wash them by hand.

I also cover the buckets after I have washed them to prevent anything from getting inside of them. My wife says I am more cautious with these materials than hospitals are with their instruments. That may be but I can feel confident consuming this milk or products we make from the milk without a worry.

A strip cup is important to use in order to preserve the quality of the milk and the taste of it. The first several squirts of milk from each goat should go into the strip cup rather than into your stainless steel bucket. Check the milk in the strip cup closely. Look for any signs of blood or clumps.

A black cup is easiest to use because you can see problems with the white milk without any trouble. I know people who use red cups and feel they work well. If you notice any problems with the milk from the goat don't consume it. Contact your vet for further evaluation.

Clean the teats of the goat before you milk them. You will find recipes for this online but most of them contain bleach. I don't use bleach on my goats. My vet tells me to use baby wipes as they are gentle and sanitary. However, they are also disposable so I don't use them.

Instead, I take old clothes or t-shirts that are clean and cut them into strips. I place a bit of sanitary hand gel on a strip, gently clean the teats, and it is done. This is very inexpensive but needs to be done.

Clean them and then squirt a few times into the strip cup. There can be plenty of bacteria in the first few squirts so don't be tempted to use them to increase the amount of milk you get from your Nigerian Dwarf goats.

If all looks well with the milk, you can start filling up the bucket. Continue to milk the goat until very little is coming out with each squirt. Next, you will need a filtering system of some kind in place for milking your goats. This is important so you can remove any hairs or other entities from the milk before you consume it.

I use a canning funnel and a coffee filter basket as my filtering system. It works well and you can buy these items at retailers for about $7 USD/ £5. You can also try using a milk strainer but they do require the use of disposable paper filters. I try to do what is best for the environment and not use disposable products unless I have no other options.

Your filtering system comes into play after you have milked your goat and placed the milk into the stainless steel bucket. Place a glass jar on the table, put the canning funnel in it, and the coffee filter basket on top of that. Slowly pour the milk from the bucket into the contraption.

This will remove elements from your milk. It results in the milk and only the milk going into the glass jars. Again, using plastic containers to store your goat milk can alter the taste – and not for the better.

Place a secure lid on the glass jar once it is filled up with the filtered milk. Immediately place it into the refrigerator. I label my jars of milk with a dry erase marker. I write on the glass the date I got the milk. We have a rotating system in our refrigerator so we use the oldest milk first.

Milk that doesn't get used after 5 days is given to our cats. It would likely be good much longer than that but we don't take any chances. With a busy household full of kids and a wife who loves to bake though the milk rarely doesn't get consumed by us.

Milking Machines

I know some owners who use milking machines for their goats. Typically, these are used by those who breed and have numerous goats to milk each day. They are also used by those wishing to save time or who have health concerns such as arthritis which can make milking by hand very painful.

I don't use milking machines because of the cost involved in such a device. I also don't have an abundance of goats so I can get the milking done in very little time. I also like the time with my goats as it is a bit of one on one time when we interact. I talk to them while I milk them and that helps them to be calm. It also helps with our bonding.

If you are interested in milking machines, there are quite a few options out there to consider. They usually cost $1,000 USD/£650 or more depending on the model. You can buy used ones for about half that price. Hoegger offers a good product design. Caprine Supply has a simple but effective milking machine they offer.

One of my friends was able to convert a Babson milker to use it for his Nigerian Dwarf goats. He really likes it and it was something he already had so he didn't have to go invest in another machine.

If you have goats with small teats, you may discover milking them is hard. I have been told the Maggidan Milker is great for such issues. If you have larger goats you may find the Segal Milker is the way to go. Simple Pulse gets great reviews for their product.

If you use any type of milking machine for your goats, make sure you are well versed in how to operate it. An electric vacuum milker may be useful but it can also be dangerous to your goats if you don't use it correctly. This can cause damage to the udders and the teats.

Milk Products

It isn't just milk you can enjoy from your Nigerian Dwarf goats either. You can make cheese from this delicious milk that is good for you and tastes very good. There are many recipes but the one we use in my home is to make chevre cheese. I urge you to give it a try and to decide what you like the taste of. It isn't hard to make goat cheese and it lasts for about 10 days after you make it.

We also make goat butter and it is very smooth and creamy. The butter can be used for up to 30 days after you make it. We use it to bake and cook with. We use it to spread on our bread. I can't tell you the last time we purchased milk, cheese, or butter from any grocery store.

Chapter 14 - Common Mistakes to Avoid

My goal with this book from the start has been to offer plenty of information so you can enjoy Nigerian Dwarf goats to the fullest. Giving you the information to be well informed is important so you can make good decisions. However, there are also some common mistakes with them that still happen. I figure if we dedicate this chapter to talking about them, it will help you to avoid such pitfalls as well.

Too Many Goats

I will agree with you that these Nigerian Dwarf goats are the cutest thing out there. However, too many of them to care for becomes quite a chore and expensive. You won't enjoy them and it is going to take a toll on you. Make sure you don't get in over your head.

Wrong Food Choices

Feeding your goats the wrong food items can cause serious health problems for them. Don't save a few bucks on the cost of food and then deal with huge vet bills. Keep food secure and away from the goats so they can't consume more than they should.

Water isn't Clean

Water that is clean and readily accessible to your goats is very important. Without it, they will suffer health problems. I know some owners who put huge buckets of water out there and don't refill them until they are empty. The problem is they don't clean them either.

No Protection from Predators

These precious miniature goats can become victims of injuries or death from predators. It doesn't take much effort to build a secure fence and to ensure nothing gets in there to harm them.

Failure to Offer Preventative Care

Don't wait until your goats are sick before you take care of them. Preventative care is your responsibility as an owner. Give them vaccinations, give them deworming medication, take care of their hooves, etc.

Not Training

Your Nigerian Dwarf goats need to know their boundaries. If you don't set them in place they will walk all over you. Training your goats is something you need to invest time for.

Not having Fun

Don't get so involved with the care of your goats that you forget to have fun with them. Go play with them, talk to them, have fun with them. You can even exercise them while playing so both of you benefit.

Isolation

The social needs of these goats are very high. They should only be isolated when they are recovering from an illness or they are about to give birth and need more rest. Females with young can also be isolated for a few weeks so they aren't disturbed by other goats.

Buying without Information

Never purchase these goats without finding out information about the breeder. Make sure they are legitimate and they have all the necessary paperwork to provide you with. Use the information in this book to ensure you get a fair price for the type of Nigerian Dwarf goat you wish to purchase.

Lack of Time

Not enough time means your goats are going to suffer. You can't successfully have them as pets if you don't have at least a few hours a day to tend to their needs. You can't skip days of milking them, feeding them, or interacting with them. They require the right conditions to feel comfortable and to thrive.

Goats aren't Allowed

Never keep these goats in a location where they aren't allowed. If you do so, you can end up in legal trouble and have to go to court. Your goats can be taken from you and you won't get them back. Don't keep goats in your home!

Lacking Preventative Care

Not taking care of the needs of your goats including their hooves, vaccines, and other forms of preventative care will get you into trouble. Your goats will get sick or die. You will have high costs too for treatment from your vet.

Not Securing the Environment

Always watch your goats and look for any signs that they may be trying to get out. Check your fencing regularly to make sure they can't get out and predators can't get in. You can't let them get loose or there is the risk of harm coming to them.

Not Enough Information

A lack of information or the wrong information can cause you plenty of concerns with your goats. You can't just learn as you go, you need to be well prepared with a solid plan of action before you get them. Since you are reading this book, you will have the right information at your fingertips and that is a plus!

Not Knowing the Normal Vitals for your Goats

It can be difficult to know if your goat has a temperature or if they have some other health issue if you don't know what is normal. These are the vitals for your goats that you need to memorize:

- Temperature should be between 102 and 104 F
- Pulse should be between 70 and 80 beats per minute
- Breathing should be from 15 to 30 times per minute
- Rumen movements could be active and you should hear such movement every 1 or 2 minutes

Not Understanding Puberty and Growth

Nigerian Dwarf goats will reach puberty when they are about ¾ fully grown. This can be as early as 3 months for the bucks and between 12 and 18 months for the doe population. It takes about 2 or 3 years for them to reach their full size. They will reach their full height, then depth, and then width.

Not Preventing Pregnancy

If you want to breed your goats for offspring, do so. However, you need to remember they can breed any time of the year. If you don't separate your adult males from your adult females you are going to end up with far more offspring than you imagined or wanted. With up to 4 kids per pregnancy, you can see how it would become a factor to contend with.

Chapter 15 - Conclusion

If you have read my book from start to finish, you have all the details you need to get started with Nigerian Dwarf goats. You realize they take time and energy to care for but they are so much fun and well worth it. You have realistic information about what their daily care and ongoing care needs happen to be. You also have information about housing them and feeding them.

These goats make amazing pets for your family to enjoy. We wouldn't know what to do without ours. Each of them has a unique personality and it is fun to interact with them. Make sure you find a wonderful breeder to buy your goats from. Don't be in a rush to get them and then discover you have sick animals, the papers aren't completed, or you paid too much for them.

One of the perks of having Nigerian Dwarf goats around is the milk they provide. It is beyond delicious and you will likely find you don't want to drink anything else. You can also use it for baking and for cooking and it will enhance the taste of anything you make with it.

No matter how tempting it may be, don't overlook their vaccines and other needs. If you do so, it will cost you more money in the end then just taking care of those important needs. It is your responsibility to make sure you follow all of the laws and regulations where you live regarding ownership of Nigerian Dwarf goats.

They can make a good meal for various predators so make sure their shelter doesn't allow them to get out or for predators to gain access. With proper care and shelter there is very little risk of injury, illness, or death for your goats. If you are negligent in any of these areas though it does allow for negative things to happen and to destroy the herd you have created.

Daily exercise is good for your goats, so make sure they are getting it. Watch their diet to ensure it has the right balance of nutrients for them. Fresh water access is very important for their well-being. Since goats are social they need to interact with you and with other goats on a daily basis. You can take them for walks on a leash or give them toys to play with in order to ensure they do get plenty of exercise.

Learning how to successfully milk the mature females does take time. Don't be intimidated by the process. Instead, give it the time it needs early on and you will improve. Don't skip milking days unless it is almost time for a female to give birth. Otherwise, you should be milking in the morning and again at night.

Each of your miniature goats will need at least 10 square feet of space. Make sure the area is going to remain dry and well ventilated. It should offer them shade when it is hot and warm areas when it is cold. It should protect them from all the elements including the wind, rain, and snow.

You can build a structure from scratch or you can convert a barn or even a shed into something you can use. While it may be tempted to use a dirt floor, that isn't a good idea if you live in a region where there is often moisture including rain and snow. The dirt won't drain well and this can increase the risk of bacterial infections and other health concerns for your goats.

I use stone dust and it is a very good option. It is inexpensive and it is also very easy to clean. Avoid facing the entrance of the goat shelter to the North as that makes it too easy for the wind to be a problem as it will blow in there all winter long. Provide them with an outdoor section and an indoor section so they can decide where they will hang out based on temperature and other factors.

Always keep the stalls clean to prevent odors and to prevent health risks for your Nigerian Dwarf goats. The cleanlier their environment is the healthier they are going to be. The bacteria from feces is a huge factor and you want to avoid it. Make sure the goats all have enough space too and they aren't overcrowded.

The bedding area should offer shavings for your goats all year long. This will help the stalls to stay fresh smelling. I use a pitchfork weekly to fluff the shavings for them. I change the shavings once a month.

When it comes to the outdoors spacing, you should have at least 130 square feet per goat. Make sure the fencing is durable and it isn't going to allow them to escape. Cable ties and t-posts can help to secure the fencing more than normal.

While it should be self-explanatory, don't overlook the importance of fresh water that is clean for your goats at all times. They won't drink much at once but they will drink frequently through the day. Females who are lactating will consume twice as much water as the other goats.

Goats can often knock over water buckets so don't place them on the ground. They should be hung up so they can easily reach them. Place several of them in a given area too so they don't have to fight over access to the same one. With warmer temperatures, you may need to add ice to the water so it stays cool until the next time you change it.

During the winter months, make sure you don't have water which is inaccessible due to a layer of ice forming. There are water buckets that can be plugged in which are a good idea. They have a coil wrap around the cords too so you don't have to worry about the goats chewing on the cord and getting shocked.

Goats enjoy being brushed and scratched. Using a stiff brush you need to get rid of all the dirt and mud that has accumulated on them that day or from the night before. I tend to brush my goats in the morning but other people like to do it at night. You can decide on the schedule, just make sure you are consistent with it. In the summer, clip the coat to keep them cool, reduce the risk of mites and lice, and to help their new coat grow back thick and shiny.

Every 3 months you need to take care of the hooves for your Nigerian Dwarf goats. Clean out each hoof with the pointed part of sharp shears. Trim the side walls so they are level with the sole. Remember to do this slowly and only to take off a small amount of the hoof at a time. This will prevent you from going too far down.

For safety, always take care of the hooves with the shears pointed away from your body. I can't tell you the number of times a goat I was trimming jerked or kicked. If I had the sheers pointed the other way, they would have done some serious damage to my mid section. By trimming sideways, you can make the sole and the heels flush.

Trimming close to the start of winter weather is recommended. This will reduce the chances of the mud and debris getting caught in the hooves. When it is in there and remains for a period of time, foot rot will develop. This can disable or kill your goat.

Goats never really like to have the feet handled but you need to do it. Start this process when they are very young so they get used to it and they will tolerate it. Don't hold the hoof up any higher than the knee of the goat.

Always work with your vet to create a vaccine and deworming schedule for your goats. This type of preventive care is essential for their day to day health and well-being. I also give my goats a copper supplement every 6 months. They should get 1 gram for up to 22 pounds of body weight.

They don't like the taste so I had it in large marshmallows. These goats love that as a treat. It is a hassle free way to get them to take the supplement. You will be able to tell when your goats just aren't feeling like they should. The more observe and interact with them daily the easier it will be to identify anything out of the ordinary.

Do what you can to keep them healthy and to help them recovery from any illness. Work closely with a vet you trust to take care of problems outside of your ability to resolve. Sometimes, you will only have a matter of hours to get them treatment so don't drag your feet.

Follow the guidelines for successful buying and selling of Nigerian Dwarf goats. Most of the buyers and sellers out there are legitimate but that isn't always going to be the case. Do your homework and report anything that seems out of the ordinary. The proper authorities can investigate it from there and take any action they feel needs to be put in motion to remedy the situation.

Use common sense and good management to help you get your goats and to have a wonderful experience with them. Preventative care is very important to make sure your goats have a low risk of health problems or issues with nutritional well-being. They need ample room for living and the need to be interacted with often.

Consider if you are ready for the thrill and the responsibility of Nigerian Dwarf goats. If you are, there isn't any better time to start assessing your location and what you can offer for housing and shelter. Don't shop for the goats until you have everything in place for them. Doing so will cut down on the problems you experience when you bring them home.

I hope you have found this book to be very enlightening and entertaining. I have enjoyed sharing with you the ins and outs of caring for Nigerian Dwarf goats. You should have all the information you need now to make a well informed decision.

Perhaps you have decided the goats are amazing but not something you can realistically care for. Hopefully, you have decided they are exactly what you are looking for and you are soon going to be adding them to your household as pets!

Chapter 16 – Websites and Resources

When it comes to Nigerian Dwarf goats, there are several official resources you can turn to. These are the most common where you can register them, share information, and ask questions.

AGA – American Goat Society
http://www.americangoatsociety.com/

The American Goat Society, known as AGA, was established in 1935. It continued to grow and in 1937 it joined forces with the International Dairy Goat Record Association. As a result, there pedigree records more than 80 years old. They can help you if you need to research the family history of your Nigerian Dwarf goats.

AGA accepts registrations for your goats based on the documents you provide. They offer very reasonable prices for the registry listing. The full list of applicable fees is found on their website.

They are also a great resource if you have questions. I contacted them several times when we first got our goats and they always helped me. They were always patient and explained the information in terms that were easy for me to understand and follow.

I love AGA because they are always open to feedback. They continue to strive to make it a great association to belong to. They always put the care and needs of these goats as the priority. If you share you feedback with them they can use it to continue moving forward and offering the very best practices for all of us.

ADGA – American Dairy Goat Association https://adga.org/

Since 1904 the American Dairy Goat Association, ADGA, has been offering services. They have more than 2 million goats registered so it is a quite a valuable entity. Members are able to enjoy reduced fees for each goat they register. Their websites provides a full list of their services and fees.

There are also ADGA scholarships available which you may be interested in looking at. I have only just begun to look at what is offered, how to apply, and the requirements. There is so much competition out there for athletic scholarships and community scholarships. I figured as my kids get closer to graduation we can apply for those that have to do with our goats.

If you are interested in taking your Nigerian Dwarf goats around to various shows to compete, you definitely want to be a member of ADGA. Their website conveniently provides a full schedule of the various events. You can find out when they will be held, requirements, and the forms to complete if you wish to sign up for any of those listed events.

ABGA – American Boer Goat Association http://abga.org/

I didn't know about American Boer Goat Association, ABGA, until we had our miniature goats for several years. I have found it to be a very good resource for me to check into now and then. They provide plenty of educational details. If you are new to raising Nigerian Dwarf goats, you will find their website to be very useful.

They host various seminars that you may be interested in being involved in. Many of them are in various locations and you have to sign up in advance due to limited space. They are branching out now to also offer some web based information programs. It is nice to be able to view them from the privacy of my home.

ANDDA – American Nigerian Dwarf Dairy Association http://www.andda.org/

My favorite resource though is American Nigerian Dwarf Dairy Association, ANDDA. Since they are focused on our specific goats, I go to them first for the information I seek. It is also a great place to meet others who also raise these goats as pets or for breeding purposes.

This is an excellent resource site to use if you are interested in buying Nigerian Dwarf goats. They have a directory of each breeder that meets or exceeds the required standards. They have them listed by state so it is easy enough to find them in your state or boarder states to check into.

Other sites, including UK sites:

www.cornerstonefarm.net
http://www.stackyard.com/pedigree/goats/breeders.html
www.pygmygoat.co.uk
http://www.renn.co.uk/pg1.html
http://www.ashworthpygmyfarm.co.uk/
http://www.westonhallfarm.co.uk

Resource Guide

Note: Websites mentioned in this book were all live at the time of printing. However, they may no longer be live when you read this book as the internet changes rapidly. This, of course, is out of our control.

https://en.wikipedia.org

http://nigerianpygmygoats.com

http://www.oregonzoo.org

http://rosasharnfarm.com

http://www.weedemandreap.com

http://commonsensehome.com

http://www.americangoatsociety.com/

https://adga.org/

http://abga.org/

http://grasseacres.com

http://www.endofthelinefarm.com

http://www.tinyangelsfarm.com

http://www.tennesseemeatgoats.com

http://www.goldenbrookfarm.com

http://www.ansi.okstate.edu

http://www.cornerstonefarm.net

http://nigeriandwarfgoats.ning.com

http://sunflowerfarmdairy.blogspot.com/

http://mynigeriandwarfs.com/

http://www.honeysweetieacres.com

http://nigeriandwarfgoats.ning.com

http://www.dummies.com

http://www.cheesemaking.com

CPSIA information can be obtained
at www.ICGtesting.com
Printed in the USA
BVHW051338230821
614886BV00009B/849